Grand Canyon: The Complete Guide

©2004 Destination Press and its licensors
ISBN 0-9678904-1-1

Contributing Writers: James Kaiser, Peter Brewitt, John Silkey
Contributing Photographers: James Kaiser, Peter Bohler
Copy Editor: Carrie Petree

Special thanks to Tom Pittenger, Lon Ayers, Dawn O'Sickey, Colleen Hyde, Ginger Reeve, Gray Thompson, and the entire staff at Grand Canyon National Park.

To order additional copies visit destinationpress.com or email
sales@destinationpress.com

Notice a change?

At Destination Press we take great pride in the accuracy of the information we provide. However, names, phone numbers, and other information do change. If you encounter a change while using this guide, please contact us. If you're the first to alert us to the change we'll send you a free copy of our revised guide!
changes@destinationpress.com

Have a great photo of Grand Canyon?
Submit it to Destination Press!!!

Destination Press is proud to accept photo submissions from talented readers/photographers like you. If your photo is selected, we'll publish it in future editions of this guide.
For more information visit www.destinationpress.com

Printed in China

GRAND
CANYON

• THE COMPLETE GUIDE •

DESTINATION PRESS

161 N. SECTION ST.
FAIRHOPE, AL 36532

4

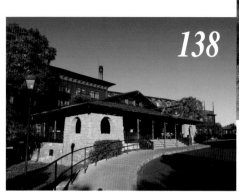

don't

EL TOVAR HOTEL
One of the finest lodges in any national park.

180 **BRIGHT ANGEL TRAIL**
The most popular route to the bottom of the canyon.

29 **COLORADO RIVER TRIPS**
Whitewater adventures through the heart of Grand Canyon.

miss out

Top Attractions at Grand Canyon N.P.

318 **HAVASU**
Gorgeous waterfalls in a secluded side canyon.

284 **CAPE FINAL**
One of the best day hikes on the North Rim.

158 **MOHAVE POINT**
Stunning views from the South Rim.

CONTENTS

FROM THE EDITOR

THE GRAND CANYON. It's America's most famous national park and one of the most impressive landmarks in the world. It's a mile deep, ten miles wide, and clearly visible from space. As a monument of nature, it has few rivals.

My first introduction to the Grand Canyon came watching National Lampoon's *Vacation*. I was just a kid, laughing in the theater as the Griswald family bumbled west to Wally World (a kind of postmodern twist on Manifest Destiny). Moments after arriving at the Grand Canyon, Chevy Chase robs the cash register at the El Tovar hotel. He then runs out to the rim to gather his family. "Alright, let's go!" he shouts. His wife protests. Dejected, Chevy stares out into the canyon for a few seconds and looks back at his wife. "Alright," he says, "let's go!"

That was my introduction. Comedy? Absurdity? Well, the first white men to set eyes on the Grand Canyon did pretty much the same thing. Four centuries ago, Spanish explorers stumbled upon the canyon while searching for a city of gold. After taking a quick look—and finding no gold—they headed to their next destination.

Incredibly, most visitors continue to make the same mistake today. They step out of their cars, take in the view, and run off to their next stop. Vegas? Check. Hoover Dam? Check. Grand Canyon? Check. One of the most incredible places on earth and they missed it!

That's where this book comes in.

From river trips to scenic flights, the Grand Canyon has it all. But it can be an incredibly overwhelming place. *Grand Canyon: The Complete Guide* breaks it down, shows you the best of what the Grand Canyon has to offer, and equips you with everything you need to know to make the most of your time in the park. So go for a hike, drive along the rim, or feast on a gourmet meal at a historic lodge. But whatever you do, don't be the Griswalds! Don't miss out on the Grand Canyon. And don't leave anything less than captivated by our most famous national park.

James Kaiser
Founder, Editor-in-Chief
Destination Press

ADVENTURES
CANYON HIKING

S IMPLY PUT, THE Grand Canyon offers some of the best hiking in America. The range of scenery in the park is incredible—from cool pine forests, to narrow slot canyons, to everything else in between. There are trails that skirt the edge of the rim and trails that plunge thousands of feet to the Colorado River. And don't forget the canyon's 2 billion years of amazing geology, arranged chronologically for your viewing pleasure.

Sound too good to be true? Not at all. But before you hit the trail, there are some important things you need to know. First, there are two types of hikes in the Grand Canyon: day hikes and backcountry (overnight) hikes. Day hikes are very straightforward—just pick a hike and go. No special permits are required. Backcountry hikes, on the other hand, require a bit more planning. Due to the overwhelming number of visitors who want to go on backcountry hikes each year, the National Park Service limits the total number of backcountry hikers allowed on each trail. Backcountry hikers must apply for permits ahead of time, which are granted on a first-come, first-served basis. Not everyone who wants a permit gets one. But permits aren't too hard to come by if you apply for them well in advance. Even during peak tourist season, same-day permits are sometimes available due to cancellations

Unlike most hikes on the planet, the trails at Grand Canyon start at the top and end at the bottom. This "mountain in reverse" style of hiking leads to some unique challenges. For one, a hike into the canyon seems deceptively easy on the way down. Keep in mind that it takes about twice as long to hike up as it takes to hike down. And then there's the temperature. The lower you go, the hotter it gets, with temperatures as much as 20°F hotter at the bottom of the canyon. Despite these challenges, hiking in the Grand Canyon is an experience not to be missed. Just follow the rules and tips on the following pages to plan a safe and memorable trip.

BEST SOUTH RIM HIKES: p.115   **BEST NORTH RIM HIKES: p.261**

DAY HIKES

There are two kinds of day hikes in the park: day hikes along the rim and day hikes that descend partway down the canyon along inner canyon trails. If you're looking for the widest variety of day hikes along the rim, head for the North Rim, which has about a half dozen popular trails. The South Rim only has one day hike along the rim: the Rim Trail (p.121). Day hikes that descend into the canyon follow longer trails, but turn around before reaching the bottom. If you choose a day hike into the canyon, plan ahead to give yourself plenty of time to return before sundown.

BACKCOUNTRY HIKES

If you're looking for more than a quick daytime jaunt, the Grand Canyon offers a number of spectacular backcountry hikes. All backcountry hikes start at the rim and drop down into the canyon. The elevation drop on these hikes is severe, so they are best tackled over more than one day. Overnight trails pass through terrain that the park classifies as "Backcountry." To camp in the Backcountry, you need to apply for a permit from the Backcountry Office. The Park Service has divided the backcountry into four management zones: Corridor, Threshold, Primitive, and Wild.

Trails in the Corridor zone are well maintained and equipped with modern facilities. There are three Corridor trails in the Grand Canyon: the Bright Angel Trail, the South Kaibab Trail, and the North Kaibab Trail. They are the most popular backcountry trails in the park. The Bright Angel Trail and North Kaibab Trail have developed campsites along the trail. Backcountry Rangers strongly recommend that first-time backpackers to the Grand Canyon use Corridor trails.

Threshold trails are unmaintained, but they are generally in fair condition. The two Threshold trails covered in this book are the Hermit Trail and the Grandview Trail.

The final two management zones, Primitive and Wild, cover extremely rugged terrain. The Thunder River Trail is the only Primitive zone trail covered in this book, although only part of it falls in the Primitive zone (the rest is Threshold). Considerable Grand Canyon hiking experience is necessary in Primitive and Wild zones.

The backcountry is also divided into "use areas" delineated on commercial maps. Knowing which use area a trail traverses is a necessary part of applying for a backcountry permit. Camping in the Corridor, Hermit, Monument, Horseshoe Mesa, and Tapeats Use Areas is limited to designated campsites or campgrounds only, and camping in these campgrounds is limited to two nights per hike. (From November 15 to February 28, however, you can camp up to four nights in popular corridor campgrounds.)

BACKCOUNTRY PERMITS

Because the National Park Service limits the total number of visitors allowed to camp in the backcountry, permits are required for all backcountry hikers. Each year, the park service receives about 30,000 requests for about 13,000 available permits. Although these numbers seem intimidating, a permit isn't too hard to come by if you plan well in advance. On short notice, however, permits can be hard to obtain, especially in the summer months.

Backcountry permits are issued by the Backcountry Reservation Office. The earliest that a permit may be requested is on the first day of the month, four months prior to the proposed start date. Permit requests can be submitted via mail or fax, but are considered late if not received at least three weeks prior to the proposed start date. The backcountry permit request form is available on the Grand Canyon's Web site. Permit requests are processed in the order they are received. All written requests are responded to via U.S. Mail (allow at least three weeks for processing).

Although most people request permits well ahead of time, cancellations sometimes make same-day permits available. You can place yourself on a waiting list for same-day permits if you arrive at the Backcountry Information Center by 8am on the day you would like to hike. For more information on backcountry permits, visit www.nps.gov/grca/backcountry/permit_app.htm or call 928-638-7875 Monday–Friday, 1pm–5pm.

The South Rim Backcountry Office is located to the east of Maswik Lodge, next to the railroad tracks. Mailing address:

Grand Canyon National Park
Backcountry Information Center
PO Box 129
Grand Canyon, AZ 86023
Fax: 928-638-2125

FEES

There is a non-refundable $10 fee per permit, plus $5 per person per night. Permit cancellations are subject to a $10 cancellation fee. Frequent hikers may wish to purchase a one-year Frequent Hiker membership for $25 that waives the initial $10 fee for each permit. If a permit is cancelled three days or more before the start date, the $5 per person fee can be applied to a future hike.

HIKING TIPS

Don't hike from the rim to the river and back in a single day

Each year, the park service rescues hundreds of day hikers stranded in the canyon. Hiking to the river and back seems deceptively easy on the way down, and by the time a weary hiker realizes how difficult the hike back up will be it's often too late. On top of the added hassle for both hikers and park rangers, evacuations can be extremely expensive for the person being evacuated. A helicopter evacuation can cost upward of $3000 per flight. By planning ahead and understanding the trail, you can easily avoid a needless evacuation.

Bring plenty of water

The biggest dangers on the trail are not scorpions, rattlesnakes, or mountain lions (in fact, these animals pose relatively little threat), but dehydration, heat exhaustion, and heat stroke. In the sweltering summer months this danger becomes even more pronounced. Temperatures rise as you descend into the canyon. The average temperature difference between the river and the rim is more than 20°F. The best way to stay safe is to avoid hiking during the middle of the day and to drink plenty of water. Rangers recommend drinking a gallon a day in the summer. Drink small amounts often, even when you don't feel thirsty. (By the time you feel thirsty you're already dehydrated.) Although some trails have access to water, many do not. Make sure you're aware of water availability on a trail before you start hiking.

Bring plenty of food

Just as important as drinking is eating. Salty snacks replace electrolytes (salts) that the body loses through sweating. If you drink water but do not replace electrolytes, you run the risk of developing hyponatremia that can lead to seizures and death. Eat much more than you usually do, and eat small amounts often. Every time you drink, you should also eat.

Take regular breaks

Not only will this give you a chance to enjoy the fine views, it will make you a more efficient hiker. Resting for five to seven minutes can remove up to 30 percent of the waste products that build up in your legs while hiking.

Use common sense

Don't take shortcuts, don't approach wild animals, and don't engage in reckless behavior. By using common sense and taking a few moments to consider your actions, your Grand Canyon experience will be that much more enjoyable.

HIKING IN THE SUMMER

Summer is the busiest hiking season in the Grand Canyon, it's also the hottest time of the year. Summer temperatures can top 110°F on many Grand Canyon trails, posing significant risks to hikers. such as:

HEAT EXHAUSTION: the result of dehydration due to intense sweating.

HEAT STROKE: a life-threatening condition caused when the body's heat-regulating mechanisms become overwhelmed. Symptoms include flushed face, dry skin, weak and rapid pulse, high body temperature, poor judgment, and unconsciousness. Heatstroke victims must be cooled immediately—move the victim to shade and continuously pour water on the victim's head and torso.

HYPONATREMIA: The result of low sodium in the blood caused by drinking too much water, not eating enough salty foods, and losing salt through sweating. Early symptoms mimic those of heat exhaustion.

With careful planning, the dangers above can be avoided. One of the easiest preventative measures is to avoid hiking in the middle of the day when temperature are at their highest. Instead, hike in the early morning and late afternoon. By resting in the shade during the middle of the day, you will limit your exposure to the scorching rays of the sun. While hiking, a good way to stay cool is to keep your clothing wet. A wet T-shirt, hat, or bandana around your neck will work wonders to cool you down.

DRINKING WATER

You should always bring your own water when hiking, but water sources are sometimes available on Grand Canyon trails. The Backcountry Office maintains a list of seasonal water sources and updates the list based on the reports of rangers and hikers. Piped water is seasonally available on the Bright Angel and North Kaibab Trails, and does not need to be treated. Water taken from creeks, springs, or the Colorado River should always be treated and purified. Water can be treated and purified in one of three ways:

• Filtering: Filter the water through a 1-micron filter, available at outdoor stores.

• Disinfecting: Use two drops of bleach or five drops of tincture of iodine per gallon of water. Allow the water to sit for 30 minutes before drinking.

• Boiling: Water should be boiled for one minute, plus one additional minute for every 1,000 feet above sea level.

The park service recommends filtering first, then adding chemicals. Hikers may also want to cache water on a trail to ensure enough water on the hike out. Try to place cached water in the shade, and mark it with your name and expected retrieval date.

HIKING HAZARDS

Lightning

Lightning storms, especially in the summer, can sweep through the Grand Canyon at a moment's notice. If you find yourself caught in a lightning storm, head to a low-lying area away from cliff edges, lone trees, or metal objects. Do not seek shelter in an area that could be subject to flash floods. While shallow overhangs may offer protection from rain, they will not offer protection from lightning and should be avoided.

Rockfalls

Rockfalls are most common during and after downpours. It is especially important to watch and listen for rockfalls during this time. Do not stand at places where rocks have obviously fallen before.

Snakes, scorpions, and other wildlife

Although the Grand Canyon is home to a variety of snakes—some of which are poisonous—snakebites are rare, occurring almost exclusively to people attempting to handle snakes. Be aware of where you place your hands and feet, and if you do encounter a snake, leave it alone. If you are bitten, contact a ranger or send someone for help.

Scorpions are common in the Grand Canyon, but they are rarely seen. Although a scorpion sting is painful, it rarely causes serious health problems. The elderly and young children are the most susceptible to scorpion venom. Hikers should always shake out their boots and clothing before putting them on. Campers should always check their sleeping bags and avoid walking around barefoot in the campsite. Having a flashlight in hand after dark is also a good idea.

Most other wildlife in the park is harmless, and those animals that could be potentially dangerous (such as mountain lions) generally stay away from people.

Flash floods

Each year, flash floods kill about 200 people in the United States. The best course of action to avoid a flash flood is to avoid areas that are subject to flooding—such as stream beds, narrow canyons, and washes—especially during downpours. If you hear or see a flood coming, move to higher ground immediately. Do not try to outrun a flash flood.

"The waters that fall during a rain on these steep rocks are gathered at once into the river; they could scarcely be poured in more suddenly if some vast spout ran from the clouds to the stream itself."

—John Wesley Powell

FLASH & DEBRIS FLOODS & FLOWS

FLASH FLOODS ARE one of the greatest dangers in the Grand Canyon. Although the region is dry for much of the year, heavy rains pound the landscape in the late summer. In July, August and early September—a time referred to as the monsoon season—thunderstorms sweep through the region on an almost daily basis. These storms can dump several inches of rain in a few short hours, and the dry landscape and sparse vegetation does little to absorb the water or slow it down. (Although the ground does absorb some water, it generally acts like a dry sponge that repels water until it becomes soaked). The runoff from these storms quickly gathers in side canyons, some of which drain enormous areas. If the rain is heavy enough and the side canyon is narrow enough, a wall of water several feet high will race through the side canyon at speeds topping 23 feet *per second*. The force of this flood is so powerful that it compresses the air in front of it, sending pebbles and small rocks flying through the air in advance of the approaching wall of water.

What is most frightening about flash floods is that they can appear in side canyons when the sky is clear and sunny overhead. Storms in the region tend to be highly localized. They can dump several inches of rain over a concentrated area while the land a few miles away receives none. In the late summer of 1997, 12 tourists were hiking through Antelope Canyon not far from the Grand Canyon. As they were hiking, a thunderstorm 10 miles upstream dumped an inch and a half of rain in less than an hour. The runoff from this storm gathered with remarkable speed, sending an 11-foot wall of water roaring through Antelope Canyon. The flood killed all but one of the hikers, who had been pressed against the canyon wall as the flood surged past. By the time the flooding subsided, every article of clothing on his body except his boots had been ripped off by the sediment and grit in the water.

Similar to flash floods, but even more powerful, are debris flows. Unlike flash floods, which are 80–90 percent water, debris flows are a deadly mix of water, rocks, and sediment—up to 60 percent solid material by volume. They roar through side canyons at a maximum speed of 25 feet per second—three feet per second *faster* than flash floods—ripping out trees and sweeping away boulders weighing hundreds of tons. Although few people have ever witnessed a debris flow, they create a deafening roar that shakes the ground. On average, two debris flows are triggered in the Grand Canyon each year.

ADVENTURES
MULE
RIDES

FOR OVER A century, mule rides have been one of the Grand Canyon's most popular activities. Everyone from Teddy Roosevelt to The Brady Bunch has descended the canyon on mule, and while hardcore hikers would never dream of passing up a chance to hike into the canyon, for many people mules are the only way to go. These sure-footed animals are fun, convenient, and offer a genuine taste of the Old West. And did we mention they do most of the hard work for you?

Although less demanding than hiking, mule riding is still a physical activity. Riders must sit up straight on a moving animal for extended periods of time, which requires more endurance than you might think. Mule riding is also not for the faint of heart. Mules are incredibly safe animals, but they often walk frighteningly close to the edge of the trail. (Sometimes it seems like they're doing this intentionally just to taunt you with their amazing sense of balance.) Despite these challenges, few people have any serious problems riding mules, and most people consider the experience to be great fun.

The South Rim offers both day and overnight mule rides. Day rides head down the Bright Angel Trail to Plateau Point (p.186) and arrive back in Grand Canyon Village by midafternoon. Overnight rides follow the Bright Angel Trail all the way to the bottom where riders spend the night at Phantom Ranch (p.188). They then return the next morning via the South Kaibab Trail. Two-night rides are also available from mid-November through March. Reservations for South Rim mule trips are accepted up to a year in advance and are highly recommended for the busy summer months. The North Rim only offers day rides, including rides along the rim and rides that descend partway down the North Kaibab Trail.

No experience is necessary for a mule ride, but mule riders must be at least 4 feet 7 inches tall (1.38 m), speak fluent English, and weigh less than 200 pounds (91 kg).

SOUTH RIM MULE RIDES: p.123   NORTH RIM MULE RIDES: p.266

ADVENTURES
RIVER RUNNING

WHAT CAN WE say? A river trip through the Grand Canyon is one of the most incredible outdoor adventures in North America. And with good reason. From fighting off frothing rapids to hiking up lush side canyons to reach hidden waterfalls, river running the Grand Canyon is an experience that you'll remember for the rest of your life.

Commercial outfitters offer a number of guided river trips through the Grand Canyon. These trips, which generally cost $200–$250 per person per day, range in length from one day to three weeks. The best trips are the multi-day adventures that run between Lees Ferry (river mile 0) and Diamond Creek (river mile 226). (One- to three-day "sampler" trips run at the end of the canyon can't compare with trips run through the heart of the park.) Some companies also offer trips geared to specific interests such as hiking, photography, or natural history.

River trips are run on both motorized and non-motorized boats. Motorized trips speed through the canyon at a fast pace, allowing you to visit more sights in less time. While some people find this convenient, others regret missing out on much of what the inner canyon has to offer.

Nonmotorized boats come in two types: rafts and dories. Inflatable rafts offer a smoother ride through the rapids. Dories offer a much more tumultuous—and much more exciting—ride where flipping is a possibility, but for many people these beautiful boats are the only way to go.

The river-running season generally lasts from mid-April through early November. Summer is the busiest time, but it's also the most uncomfortable, with temperatures at the bottom of the canyon often topping 100°F. The best time to take a river trip is in the spring or the fall, when temperatures are milder and the river is much less crowded. Private, noncommercial river trips are also allowed, but the waiting time for a permit can last several years.

COLORADO RIVER TRIPS: p.28   COLORADO RIVER INFO: p.211

COMMERCIAL OUTFITTERS

Aramark-Wilderness River Adventures, Oar powered & motor raft
www.riveradventures.com, 800-992-8022, 928-645-3296

Arizona Raft Adventures, Oar powered & motor raft
www.azraft.com, 800-786-7238, 928-526-8200

Arizona River Runners, Oar powered & motor raft
www.raftarizona.com, 800-477-7238, 602-867-4866

Canyon Explorations/Expeditions, Oar powered raft
www.canyonexplorations.com, 800-654-0723, 928-774-4559

Canyoneers, Oar powered & motor raft
www.canyoneers.com, 800-525-0924, 928-526-0924

Colorado River and Trail Expeditions, Oar powered & motor raft
www.crateinc.com, 800-253-7328, 801-261-1789

Diamond River Adventures, Oar powered & motor raft
www.diamondriver.com, 800-343-3121, 928-645-8866

Grand Canyon Discovery, Inc, Oar powered raft
www.grandcanyondiscovery.com, 800-786-7238, 928-526-8200

Grand Canyon Expeditions Company, Oar powered & motor raft, dory
www.gcex.com, 800-544-2691, 435-644-2691

Hatch River Expeditions, Motor raft
www.hatchriverexpeditions.com, 800-433-8966, 435-789-3813

Moki Mac River Expeditions, Oar powered & motor raft, dory
www.mokimac.com, 800-284-7280, 801-268-6667

O.A.R.S, Oar powered raft, dory
www.oars.com, 800-346-6277, 209-736-2924

Outdoors Unlimited, Oar powered raft
www.outdoorsunlimited.com, 800-637-7238, 928-526-2852

Tour West, Oar powered & motor raft, dory
www.twriver.com, 800-453-9107, 801-225-0755

Western River Expeditions, Motor raft
www.westernriver.com, 800-453-7450, 801-942-6669

CHOOSE YOUR WEAPON

OAR-POWERED RAFT

Oar-powered rafts offer a great mix of safety and excitement. Their flexibility allows them to bounce off obstacles undamaged and absorb much of a rapid's energy, resulting in a smoother ride. Tipping is rarely a problem, but expect to get wet. Some rafts are paddled exclusively by a guide, others allow passengers to paddle.

Photo courtesy O.A.R.S

DORY

These wooden or fiberglass boats require the most skill to maneuver and are only paddled by guides. Because they ride like a roller coaster through the rapids—and occasionally flip over—dory boats are not for the timid. But they provide the most rugged, exciting, and elegant ride the Grand Canyon has to offer.

MOTORIZED J-RIG

J-Rigs are the biggest—and most stable—craft on the water. These inflatable boats accommodate up to 20 people. As a result, they transport the majority of commercial passengers through the Grand Canyon. J-Rigs speed through the canyon faster than nonmotorized boats. Depending on your preference, this can be a good or a bad thing.

Photo courtesy Western River Expeditions

ADVENTURES
SCENIC
FLIGHTS

N O MATTER HOW much time you've spent peeking over the rim of the Grand Canyon, nothing can prepare you for the perspective you'll gain from the air. Viewed from above, the canyon's labyrinth of temples and buttes seems to go on forever. The sheer magnitude of the landscape and the incredible power of erosion are revealed in a manner hard to imagine from the ground.

More than 100,000 scenic flights soar over the Grand Canyon each year. The vast majority depart from Las Vegas, Nevada, and Tusayan, Arizona (just outside the main entrance to the South Rim). Both airplane and helicopter flights are offered. The main difference between an airplane and a helicopter flight (other than a personal affinity for one or the other) is the elevation at which they fly. Air-safety regulations require airplanes to fly about 1,000 feet higher than helicopters. Most people prefer helicopter flights because they provide a closer view, but airplane flights allow you to cover more ground in less time—and often for less money.

Strict regulations govern which parts of the park may be visited by scenic flights. Over 75 percent of the park is off limits, including the area above the popular viewpoints on the North and South Rims and the "corridor zone" between them. Furthermore, no aircraft may fly below the rim within the boundaries of the park (though some flights departing from Las Vegas land below the rim on Indian reservations). Despite these restrictions, scenic flights reveal some of the most remote and beautiful parts of the canyon, many of which are seldom seen by hikers or river runners.

Scenic flights from Tusayan cost anywhere from $80 to $260, depending on the route and the carrier that you choose. In Vegas, helicopter flights generally cost $250 or more, while airplane flights cost $200 and up.

TUSAYAN FLIGHTS : p.127   **LAS VEGAS FLIGHTS: p.32**

SCENIC FLIGHT OPERATORS
(LAS VEGAS)

Air Vegas Airlines
Airplane & helicopter tours
www.airvegas.com, 800-255-7474, 702-736-3599

Casino Travel & Tours
Airplane & helicopter tours
www.casinotravel.com, 888-444-9928, 702-946-5075

Heli USA Airways
Helicopter tours
www.heliusa.com, 800-359-8727, 702-736-8787

King Airlines
Airplane & helicopter tours
www.kingairelines.com, 702-361-7811

Look Tours
Helicoptor & airplane tours
www.looktours.com, 800-566-5868, 702-233-1627

Maverick Helicopter Tours
Helicopter tours
www.maverickhelicopter.com, 888-261-4414, 702-261-0007

Papillon
Helicopter tours
www.papillon.com, 888-635-7272, 702-736-7243

Scenic Airlines
Airplane tours
www.scenic.com, 800-634-6801, 702-638-3300

Sundance
Helicopter tours
www.helicoptour.com, 800-653-1881, 702-736-0606

ADVENTURES
GC FIELD INSTITUTE

T HE GRAND CANYON Field Institute is a private organization dedicated to enhancing the understanding and enjoyment of Grand Canyon through firsthand experience. They work in partnership with the National Park Service to offer classes exploring the natural and cultural history of the Grand Canyon region through backpacking, rim walks, day hikes, river trips, and classroom instruction. Activities offered by the Grand Canyon Field Institute accomodate a wide range of ages and levels of experience. Subject matter includes:

- Geology
- Ecology
- Archaeology
- Ornithology
- Botany
- Orienteering
- History
- Photography
- Survival Skills
- Backcountry Emergency Response

The non-profit Grand Canyon Association, established in 1932, is the parent organization of the Grand Canyon Field Institute.

Contact information:

Grand Canyon Field Institute
PO Box 399
Grand Canyon, AZ 86023
phone: 866-471-4435
fax: 928-638-2484
gcfi@grandcanyon.org
www.grandcanyon.org/fieldinstitute

National Canyon

GRAND CANYON GEOLOGY

T HE GRAND CANYON is a geological wonderland. There are few locations on the planet with so many eye-popping rock formations on display in a single place. It's safe to say that, had they been located elsewhere, many of these rock formations would be world-famous landmarks on their own. But within the depths of the canyon, they occur by the dozen. Rainbow-splashed mesas, temples, and buttes cascade down from the rim, extending for miles in either direction. Visually, there is so much to see—so many colors, textures, and shadows—that your sense of perspective often melts away. The scope of the scenery is dizzying, which is what makes staring out into the Grand Canyon so much fun.

Even if you know nothing about geology, the Grand Canyon is still an impressive sight. But take the time to learn about the forces that created it, and you'll look upon the canyon with a fresh set of eyes. Suddenly, what was once amazing will become astounding. What once took your breath away will make your head spin.

On a human timescale the Grand Canyon seems ancient, peaceful, and serene. On a geologic timescale, however, it is young, violent, and exciting. Many people are shocked to discover that the Grand Canyon was created in less than 6 million years. When you consider that the earth is over 4.5 *billion* years old, 6 million years seems like the blink of an eye. It's as if northern Arizona suddenly just cracked open and—bam!—there was the Grand Canyon.

In reality, northern Arizona was sliced open by the Colorado River. After tumbling down from the Rockies, the Colorado twists and turns through the desert Southwest, picking up an enormous amount of sediment along the way. This sediment—a mixture of gravel, silt, and clay eroded from the region's soft rocks—scrapes along the bottom of the river like sandpaper, cutting downward at the rate of about 6.5 inches every 1,000 years. Over the past 5 million years, the Colorado has sliced through northern Arizona like a knife slices through a wedding cake. In the process it has exposed dozens of layers of progressively older rocks. This gives the Grand Canyon its most defining characteristic—it is one of the few places in the world where you can view almost 2 billion years of Earth history just by glancing up and down.

So the creation of the Grand Canyon was a two-step process. The first step was the initial laying down of the rock, which took hundreds of millions of years, and the second was the erosion of the canyon by the Colorado River, which took less than 6 million years. To fully understand the depth and complexity of the geology of the Grand Canyon, it helps to examine the rock-building process first.

THE GRAND CANYON'S ROCKS

MOST OF THE rocks in the Grand Canyon are sedimentary rocks, laid down over millions of years as eroded material accumulated on the surface of what would one day become northern Arizona. As oceans advanced and retreated over this ancient landscape, an extraordinary range of environments came into being. Giant sand dunes, muddy river deltas, and shallow tropical seas were all present at one time or another. Eventually the built-up sediments from each of these environments formed sedimentary rocks; sand dunes were cemented into sandstone, mud was compressed into shale, and the discarded shells of marine animals were cemented together into limestone. (A listing of these rocks is found on pages 40.)

Because the rocks in the Grand Canyon were laid down chronologically, one on top of the other, they reflect a simple geological relationship known as superposition. In its simplest terms, superposition means that the rocks above are younger than the rocks below. Move your eyes from the rim to the river, and you are essentially staring back into time. At the very bottom of the canyon, we find the region's oldest exposed rocks: Vishnu Schist and Zoroaster Granite. These rocks are referred to as the Precambrian Rocks of the Inner Gorge. They are the only common rocks in the Grand Canyon that aren't sedimentary.

Vishnu Schist is a metamorphic rock that was created 1.7 billion years ago. It formed when intense heat and pressure transformed shale into schist. About 200 million years later, magma shot up into cracks in the schist and cooled into Zoroaster Granite, which has a distinct pinkish hue. As a result, the dark Vishnu Schist is marbled with beautiful veins of pink granite.

A little over 1 billion years ago a collection of sedimentary rocks known as the Grand Canyon Supergroup started to form. These rocks were later slightly metamorphosed and tilted at a 20-degree angle, but today they are only visible in a handful of places within the canyon.

It wasn't until about 543 million years ago that the Tapeats Sandstone, the oldest major sedimentary rock in the Grand Canyon, started to form. What happened in the 1 billion years between the formation of the Vishnu Schist and the Tapeats Sandstone is a bit of a mystery. During this time, up to 12,000 feet of additional rocks formed on top of the Vishnu Schist. But by 570 million years ago these additional rocks had eroded away, leaving an enormous gap in the geologic record. Geologists refer to such a gap as an unconformity. In the Grand Canyon, the gap between the Vishnu Schist and the Tapeats Sandstone is known as the Great Unconformity (a name given by John Wesley Powell).

". . . the thought grew in my mind that the canyons of this region would be a Book of Revelations in the rock-leaved Bible of geology. The thought fructified and I determined to read the book."

– John Wesley Powell

Vishnu Schist

Tapeats Sandstone

Great Unconformity

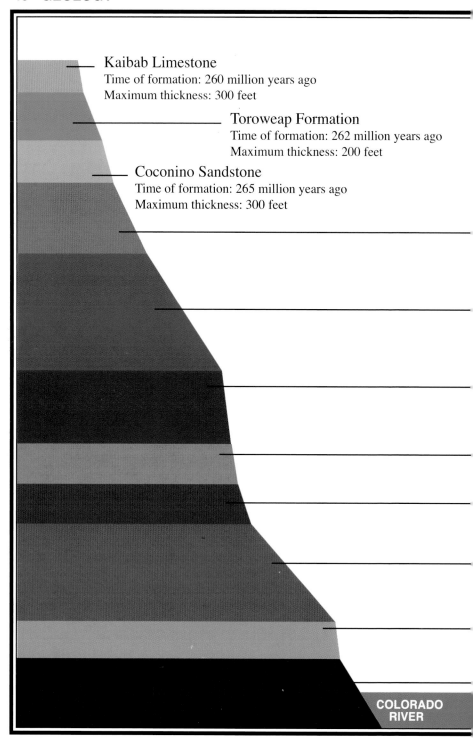

Kaibab Limestone
Time of formation: 260 million years ago
Maximum thickness: 300 feet

Toroweap Formation
Time of formation: 262 million years ago
Maximum thickness: 200 feet

Coconino Sandstone
Time of formation: 265 million years ago
Maximum thickness: 300 feet

COLORADO
RIVER

ROCKS
— *of the* —
GRAND CANYON

Hermit Shale
Time of formation: 270 million years ago
Maximum thickness: 1,000 feet

Supai Group
Time of formation: 270-320 million years ago
Maximum thickness: 1,000 feet

Redwall Limestone
Time of formation: 340 million years ago
Maximum thickness: 500 feet

Temple Butte Limestone
Time of formation: 370 million years ago
Maximum thickness: 1,000 feet

Muav Limestone
Time of formation: 530 million years ago
Maximum thickness: 800 feet

Bright Angel Shale
Time of formation: 540 million years ago
Maximum thickness: 450 feet

Tapeats Sandstone
Time of formation: 550 million years ago
Maximum thickness: 300 feet

Vishnu Schist
Time of formation: 1.7–1.5 billion years ago
Maximum thickness: 1,300 feet

Vishnu Schist

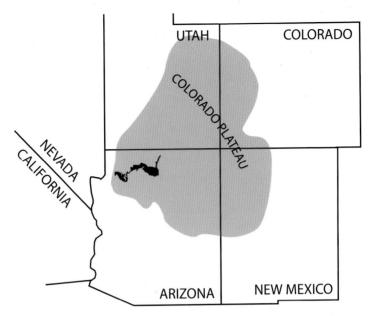

THE COLORADO PLATEAU

T HE SEDIMENTS THAT ultimately formed the sedimentary rocks in the Grand Canyon accumulated at or near sea level. So how did they end up thousands of feet *above* sea level? The answer has to do with the location of the Grand Canyon, which lies on the southwestern edge of a huge area known as the Colorado Plateau. This area—filled with some of the most stunning national parks in America—encompasses much of the Four Corners region, including parts of Arizona, Utah, Colorado, and New Mexico.

Starting about 60 million years ago, forces within the earth began pushing the Colorado Plateau upward. By about 5 million years ago, the Colorado Plateau had risen over a vertical mile. This higher elevation led to increased precipitation, which led to increased erosion that stripped away many of the region's rocks. Although the Kaibab Limestone—the top-most rock layer in the Grand Canyon—was once covered by as much as 10,000 feet of younger rocks, those rocks have since eroded away. As erosion has continued to sculpt the region, it has created one of the most stunning landscapes in the world.

Aside from their physical beauty, the sedimentary rocks of the Grand Canyon are also notable because they are so exquisitely preserved. This is due to the relative stability, geologically speaking, of the Colorado Plateau. As continents have bounced across the globe over the past 600 million years, smashing into one another and deforming the crust of the earth, the Colorado Plateau has remained sheltered from much of the action. As a result, its sedimentary layers have survived relatively intact. By contrast, the rock layers in the geologically active regions surrounding

the Colorado Plateau—such as the Great Basin and Rocky Mountains—have been severely deformed.

Some geologists believe the Colorado Plateau has resisted deformation so successfully because its crust is much thicker than the crusts of the surrounding regions. In places, the crust beneath the Colorado Plateau is up to 25 miles thick. The crust of the Great Basin, by comparison, is only 16 miles thick. So rather than buckle and break as it has been pushed upward, the Colorado Plateau has remained relatively unaltered as a single tectonic block.

The uplift of the Colorado Plateau continues today. By some estimates, it has risen as much as 1,000 feet in the past million years. And while much of the region has resisted internal deformation, there have been some notable geologic hiccups along its boundaries. In the western Grand Canyon, which lies near the boundary of the Colorado Plateau and the Great Basin, the crust is thinner and more broken. This has allowed magma to rise to the surface.

Over the past 2 million years, hundreds of volcanoes have erupted near the western Grand Canyon. At least 150 of them have resulted in lava pouring over the rim of the canyon and tumbling down to the Colorado River. As the lava cooled at the bottom of the canyon, it often formed massive dams that backed up the river for miles. The largest dam, which geologists have named Prospect Dam, was over 2,300 feet high. It created a massive reservoir that took 22 years to fill and stretched all the way back to Moab, Utah. But in as little as 20,000 years, the Colorado had destroyed Prospect Dam—a feat that speaks volumes of the power of the river.

Above: Remnants of lava flows in the western Grand Canyon

THE COLORADO RIVER

MORE THAN ANYTHING else, the Colorado River is responsible for the creation of the Grand Canyon. But that is only part of the story. The specifics are considerably more complex. Early geologists, beginning with John Wesley Powell, made the mistake of assuming that the modern river has always followed its present course. Using this as their starting point, they figured that the Colorado was entirely responsible for the creation of the Grand Canyon. The way they saw it, the river simply cut down into northern Arizona as the Colorado Plateau rose up around it.

Then, in the 1930s and '40s, geologists came to the starling conclusion that the Colorado has not always followed its present course. Although the ancestral Colorado did flow into northern Arizona—passing through the region that would one day become the eastern Grand Canyon—it avoided the western Grand Canyon entirely. Rather than flow east through Arizona, it flowed north into Utah. This created quite a problem. If the Colorado avoided the western Grand Canyon for much of its existence, how did the western Grand Canyon form?

This question has yet to be answered definitively. Much of the evidence has eroded away, so facts are hard to come by. But geologists have been able to piece together a general theory to explain what happened. It begins with the creation of a "lower" Colorado River that originated somewhere to the west of the Grand Canyon. Over time the headwaters of the lower Colorado eroded east until they reached the western edge of the Colorado Plateau. As they continued to carve away at the landscape, they came closer and closer to the upper Colorado. Then, around 5 million years ago, a critical divide was breached between the two rivers. The lower Colorado captured the upper Colorado and the upper Colorado started flowing west. At that moment, the modern river was born.

For the next 5 million years, the modern Colorado bore down into the landscape as the Colorado Plateau rose up around it—pretty much the way early geologists had envisioned it. But the river's rate of downward cutting has not been constant. In fact, it has varied considerably depending on which rocks the river has cut through. Soft sedimentary rocks, such as shale, were cut through quite rapidly. Harder sedimentary rocks, such as limestone, took much longer.

Regardless, the Colorado cut through all of the sedimentary rocks in a remarkably short period of time. By about 3.8 million years ago, the Grand Canyon was within 500 feet of its current depth. The river was now grinding through the Vishnu Schist—the hardest rock in the canyon—and its rate of downward cutting slowed. At the same time, another characteristic of the river had started to change. As the Colorado ground down obstacles that choked up the river, its grade began to level out. Because rivers with gentle grades are much less erosive than rivers with steep grades, the Colorado's rate of downward cutting was further reduced. In the past 1 million years it has cut down less than 50 feet.

This shocking fact reveals an incredible amount about the creation of the Grand

Canyon. While the Colorado drilled into northern Arizona like a power tool between 3 and 5 million years ago, it has done relatively little since then. Contrary to popular belief, the erosion of the Grand Canyon did not occur at a steady rate. Rather, it occurred in brief spurts when powerful forces pounded away at the landscape. These spurts have almost always corresponded to periods when massive obstacles—lava dams, the uplift of the Colorado Plateau—blocked an easy path for the river. In the end, it is the nature of the Colorado not just to find the path of least resistance, but to create it. This gives one pause when considering the ultimate fate of the manmade obstacles (dams) that hold back the river today.

HOW THE CANYON GOT SO WIDE

A LTHOUGH THE COLORADO River is incredibly good at cutting down, it's not so good at cutting horizontally. In fact, the river often adds inches to the riverbank by depositing sediment. Yet in places the Grand Canyon is over 10 miles wide. What's going on?

Even though the Colorado has carved out a remarkably deep channel, the width of the Grand Canyon is the result of runoff from the rim. In both cases, the mechanics are similar—gritty water grinds away at the region's soft rocks, breaking them down into sediment that is then flushed out of the canyon. But while most of the water in the Colorado River arrives from the east, runoff from the rim falls on northern Arizona in the form of rain and snow. A great deal of this precipitation ultimately flows into the canyon. In effect, the Colorado's deep channel serves as a kind of giant template, focusing much of the region's local erosion on the canyon walls.

But the rate of erosion has not been constant. The walls of the North Rim have eroded up to 10 times faster than the walls of the South Rim. This has nothing to do with the rocks that are being eroded—the two rims share the same rocks—but rather the amount of precipitation that tumbles down from each rim. Both sides of the Grand Canyon are tilted slightly to the south. As a result, precipitation that falls on the North Rim runs into the canyon, while precipitation that falls on the South Rim runs away from the canyon. Because the walls of the North Rim receive so much more runoff, they have eroded at a significantly faster rate. This fact is readily apparent to anyone who has visited both sides of the canyon. Viewed from the South Rim, the North Rim gradually recedes into the distance. But viewed from the North Rim, the walls of the South Rim appear as a sheer cliff.

While the rims have eroded at different rates, they both trace a jagged path to the river. Rather than descend steadily, the canyon walls cascade down in a series of craggy temples and buttes. Once again, this is due to varying rates of erosion. Just as the Colorado has cut down through the canyon's rocks at different rates, the same rocks have eroded horizontally at different rates as well. Soft rocks erode easily to form gentle slopes. Hard rocks resist erosion to form steep cliffs. This stair step formation of rock layers is one of the defining characteristics of the Grand Canyon. To frequent hikers, the varying slopes provide a constant reminder of where one is

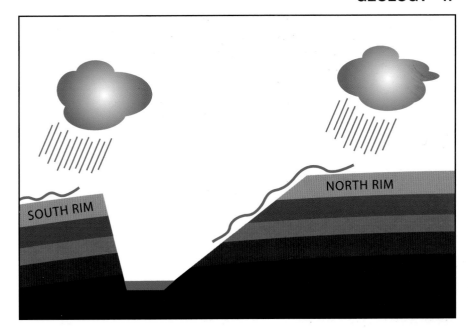

in the canyon.

Another notable geologic feature is the presence of massive side canyons, which often form along faults where the land has lifted or subsided. This creates a narrow channel where runoff accumulates. Over time, this runoff carves out a deep canyon in a self-reinforcing process. As the side canyons grow bigger and bigger, they collect more and more runoff, which leads to bigger side canyons, and so on.

Although flowing water is the main form of erosion in the Grand Canyon, other forces are also at work. One of the most notable is a process called frost wedging. It occurs when water freezes and expands in the cracks of rocks. This expansion produces incredible pressures—up to 20,000 pounds per square inch—that can split rocks apart. In some cases, frost wedging triggers rockfalls that send massive chunks of the landscape tumbling down the canyon walls.

Rockfalls also occur when soft rock layers erode beneath hard rock layers. This creates a pronounced overhang that ultimately collapses under its own weight. Such a vertical collapse is referred to as slab failure. In the canyon, with its many alternating layers of hard and soft rocks, slab failure is quite common, and it is the reason why hard rock layers erode to form steep cliffs.

In the end, the creation of the Grand Canyon was due to many things. Billions of years of rock building, erosion, and tectonic forces conspired to create the stunning landscape now on display. Millions of years from now, the same forces will have altered the Grand Canyon beyond recognition. So consider yourself lucky. You're alive at a time when you can explore and learn about one of the great geological wonders of the world. Don't squander that opportunity!

GRAND CANYON
ECOLOGY

MORE SUBTLE THAN the Grand Canyon's geology, but equally fantastic, is the park's ecology. Although first-time visitors often assume the canyon is barren and lifeless, this is anything but the case. Over 8,000 feet of sudden elevation change has created a stunning range of life zones lying remarkably close to one another. Nowhere is this more apparent than on the North Kaibab Trail. The trail starts out in a cool boreal forest on the North Rim and ends up in the scorching desert at the bottom of the canyon. In a matter of hours, hikers pass by spruce trees and cacti—the equivalent of traveling from Canada to Mexico in a single day.

The wide range of biodiversity in the Grand Canyon is due, more than anything else, to the canyon's dramatic elevation change, a condition that affects both temperature and precipitation. Generally speaking, temperatures rise and aridity increases as you descend into the canyon. From the rim to the river, the contrast between environments can be extreme. At the sweltering bottom of the western Grand Canyon, an average of six inches of rain falls a year, and only rugged desert plants such as cacti and yucca can survive. The cool, high plateaus of the North Rim, however, often receive over 30 inches of precipitation a year and are covered with lush alpine forests.

Not surprisingly, these striking contrasts have also affected the distribution of animals. Cold-blooded reptiles that thrive in the warm inner canyon are much less common on the rim, and rim dwellers that require a steady source of water would fare poorly in much of the arid inner canyon. But in many cases, plants have an even greater affect on the distribution of animals than climate. Plants form the foundation of a healthy food chain and play a vital role in determining which animals live in a particular area. Plants also provide valuable habitat for animals—from birds nesting in trees to desert critters resting in the shade of desert plants.

But plants are also dependent on animals. In any ecosystem, all life forms exist in a continuous cycle of interdependence, with each organism affecting the lives of all others. A good example of this is the relationship between pinyon pines and a bird called the pinyon jay. Pinyon pines produce large seeds that, unlike some plant seeds, are too heavy to be dispersed by the wind. They are, however, a staple of the pinyon jay's diet. After gathering the nuts, the bird buries them for later use. Those seeds left uneaten will often grow into new trees. So while pinyon pines provide the jays with an important source of food, pinyon jays ensure a healthy population of pines.

When viewed as a whole, the plants and animals in a particular area form unique, interdependent communities that ecologists call biotic communities. From tropical rain forests to frozen Arctic tundra, biotic communities are found in every corner of the world. Within the Grand Canyon, we find six major biotic communities: boreal forests, ponderosa forests, pinyon-juniper woodland, desert scrub, and the lush riparian habitat along the banks of the Colorado River. With the exception of the riparian habitat, which meanders with the river along the bottom of the canyon, these biotic communities generally form horizontal bands across the Grand Canyon.

Because elevation has such a profound affect on climate, it seems reasonable to assume that biotic communities could be mapped out based on elevation. But this is not the case. Although elevation can provide a rough approximation of where certain biotic communities will occur, many other local environmental factors come into play. And many plants and animals live in more than one biotic community, creating considerable overlap. In the Grand Canyon, where a large number of biotic communities are packed into a relatively small space, the distinction between them becomes even fuzzier.

Adding to this complexity are microclimates—small pockets of temperature and moisture that vary dramatically from their immediate surroundings. Microclimates are caused by a variety of environmental factors including local topography, proximity to water, and exposure to sunlight. For example, south-facing slopes receive much more sunlight than north-facing slopes, making them significantly warmer and drier even at higher elevations. This explains why desert plants such as yucca are found growing high up the walls of the south-facing North Rim. The reverse is also true. Shady pockets along the South Rim support small populations of Douglas-fir, a tree that generally avoids the warmer, drier South Rim. These pockets shelter much cooler environments where soil tends to stay moist throughout the year.

Air currents are another cause of microclimates. During the day, as the sun beats down on the region, hot air rises up the canyon walls. At night, cool air flows down from the rim. These invisible rivers of air allow a wide range of plants to migrate up

C. HART MERRIAM

OUR CURRENT conception of biotic communities was first developed at the Grand Canyon over a century ago. In 1889 C. Hart Merriam, then director of the U.S. Biological Survey, traveled to northern Arizona to study the region's remarkable natural diversity. As he descended the canyon, Merriam came to the conclusion that different temperatures support different communities of plants and animals. He referred to these communities as life zones. Although additional research would show that life zones are dependant on much more than temperature alone, Merriam's Grand Canyon expedition marked the first time a scientist had studied plants and animals living *together* in a quantifiable way. His work paved the way for much of our current understanding of ecology.

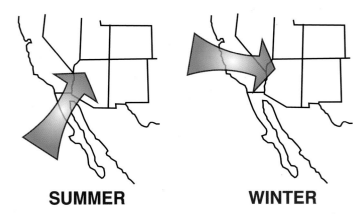

SUMMER   **WINTER**

WEATHER IN GRAND CANYON

BECAUSE THE GRAND Canyon is located in the arid Southwest, it receives much less precipitation than many other parts of the country. What little precipitation does fall arrives in the winter and summer months in a roughly 50/50 split.

In the summer, prevailing winds arrive from the south, bringing moisture from the Gulf of California and the Gulf of Mexico. Along the way, this air is lifted up and over the highlands to the south of the Grand Canyon, arriving at the canyon cooled and condensed. As the morning sun heats the inner canyon, hot air rises up and collides with the cool, moist air above. This sudden collision creates short-lived afternoon thunderstorms. In July, August, and early September, these storms pound the Grand Canyon on an almost daily basis.

In the winter, prevailing winds arrive from the west or northwest, bringing moist air from the Pacific. But much of this moisture is wrung out by the Sierra Nevada Mountains. What little moisture remains eventually finds its way to northern Arizona. Although winter storms in the Grand Canyon are much less intense than summer storms, they often linger over the canyon for several days at a time.

In the spring and the fall, the Grand Canyon is an extremely arid place, and temperature swings can be dramatic. During the day, the lack of moisture in the air allows up to 90 percent of solar radiation to reach the ground. (Humid areas, by contrast, only receive about 40 percent.) At night, the situation is reversed. Ninety percent of the canyon's accumulated heat is radiated back into the atmosphere through clear, dry skies. (In humid areas, heat is often reflected back by cloud cover.)

ICE AGE IN GRAND CANYON

JUST AS FASCINATING as the current ecology of the park is the ecology that existed here in prehistoric times. Twenty thousand years ago, during the last Ice Age, the Grand Canyon was a much different place. Although the topography was similar, the park would have been unrecognizable to modern visitors in many ways. Because the climate of the Southwest was much cooler and wetter during the Ice Age, the canyon's life zones were pushed down to lower, warmer elevations. Juniper trees grew along the banks of the Colorado River, and Douglas-fir, a tree currently found only in the park's highest elevations, grew on the Tonto Platform 3,000 feet below the rim.

Many strange and wonderful prehistoric animals also roamed the Grand Canyon during this time. One of the most notable was the Shasta ground sloth. This massive, lumbering animal stood 7 feet tall and weighed up to 400 pounds. In the early 1930s, scientists discovered preserved sloth dung in the back of several caves in the western Grand Canyon. Other prehistoric animals that lived in the region included camels, horses, and Merriam's teratorn, a bird with a wingspan of more than 12 feet! But around 10,000 years ago, all of these animals became extinct—most likely due to overhunting by early human settlers.

As the glaciers that covered much of North America retreated between 15,000 and 10,000 years ago, the Ice Age drew to a close. Temperatures rose and plants began climbing up the canyon's walls. This remarkable migration—first down, then back up the canyon—is a powerful reminder that the park's seemingly fixed life zones are highly dynamic and adaptable.

and down the canyon walls, existing in combinations that would be unlikely anywhere else.

But while life-zone boundaries are often blurred in the Grand Canyon, the canyon can also act as a formidable barrier. Consider the Abert squirrel. This small, grayish squirrel is entirely dependent on ponderosa pines as a source of food and lives exclusively in ponderosa forests. During the last Ice Age, when the climate was much cooler and wetter, ponderosa forests stretched across much of northern Arizona including the inner Grand Canyon. This gave the Abert an extensive range. But when temperatures started to rise around 10,000 years ago, the ponderosas retreated to higher elevations. Trees growing within the Grand Canyon moved up to the rims, and with them came the Abert squirrels. Some squirrels retreated to the South Rim and some retreated to the North Rim, creating two isolated populations on either side of the canyon. Over time, the squirrels living on the North Rim developed unique physical characteristics—most notably a striking white tail—that have led scientists to classify them as a separate subspecies called the Kaibab squirrel.

The interaction between plants, animals, and landscapes is incredibly complex in any environment. In the Grand Canyon, one of the most complex and dynamic environments in the world, that complexity is brought to new heights. At times, it can be a bit overwhelming. Even seasoned naturalists sometimes find themselves struggling to comprehend the sophisticated ecology of the park. But because the Grand Canyon is such a unique microcosm of North American life, it presents a tremendous opportunity for study and exploration. You could easily spend a lifetime learning about the ecology of the park, which is what keeps many people coming back year after year.

FERAL BURROS

Not all animals in the canyon are native to the region. When miners abandoned their search for riches in the Grand Canyon in the late 1800s, they often left burros behind. These pack animals, originally from the deserts of Africa, were rugged enough to survive on their own, and they quickly bred and multiplied. By 1980 there were as many as 350 feral burros in the Grand Canyon. Around this time, conservation groups became concerned that the burros were depleting the canyon's resources and threatening the livelihood of bighorn sheep. A plan was proposed to shoot the remaining burros, but an animal-protection association stepped in to rescue them. The burros were rounded up one by one, removed from the canyon, and placed up for adoption. Still, many feral burro populations remain throughout the Southwest. In recent years, there have been scattered reports of new feral burro populations in the western Grand Canyon.

BIGHORN SHEEP

Ovis canadensis

Bighorn sheep inhabit the steep cliffs of the canyon where they use their sure-footed climbing skills to avoid predators. They weigh up to 300 pounds, yet are capable of jumping down 20-foot inclines with grace. Both sexes grow horns, but the ram's are particularly impressive, twisting up and around the ears in a C-shaped curl. A large pair can weigh up to 30 pounds and reach 33 inches in length. Horns grow longer each year, but if they ever start to block peripheral vision they are *broomed*—deliberately rubbed down on rocks.

During mating season in the fall, rams establish dominance through repeated butting contests in which they charge each other head-on at speeds topping 20 miles per hour. When their horns smash together it produces a loud crack that can often be heard for miles. Thickened skulls let them withstand repeated collisions, and males with the biggest horns generally do the most mating. Over the past century, hunting and diseases from domestic sheep have taken a significant toll on bighorn populations.

U.S. RANGE

Found on rocky cliffs in the Grand Canyon

INFO

Weight: 250 pounds

Shoulder height: 3–4 feet

Length: 5–6 feet

Tracks:

BOBCAT

Lynx rufus

Bobcats are North America's most common wildcat, but they are highly elusive animals that are rarely seen or heard. They generally lay low during the day, then wander for miles at night. The bobcat is closely related to the lynx, which is larger and found in colder environments. The name *bobcat* comes from the cat's stubby "bobbed" tail.

Bobcats are slightly larger than housecats, and share many of the same personality traits. They hiss, purr, and sometimes use trees as scratching posts. Bobcats prey on a wide range of animals including deer, rabbits, squirrels, small birds, and snakes, but they rarely chase their prey. Instead, bobcats seek out a hiding spot and lie patiently in wait, pouncing when a victim approaches.

Bobcats are extremely solitary animals; males and females come together only for mating. Females usually have litters of two or three kittens, although they can have as many as seven. Recent evidence indicates that bobcat populations are stable, and may even be increasing in places.

U.S. RANGE

Found throughout the Grand Canyon

INFO

Weight: 15-30 pounds

Shoulder height: 1.5-2 feet

Length: 3-4 feet

Tracks:

ELK

Cervus elaphus

Elk are the largest member of the deer family found on the Colorado Plateau. They are distinguished from mule deer by their massive size and dark brown coloration above the neck. Although elk often appear docile, they can be dangerous during rutting season and should never be approached.

Shawnee Indians call elk *wapiti*, "White Rump," but a male elk's most distinguishing characteristic is its massive antlers. Antlers are only found on bulls. They are shed each year in the spring, and over the next three to four months new antlers grow back at the rate of about a half inch a day. Antlers can grow several feet across and weigh up to 50 pounds, reaching maximum size in time for the fall rutting season. During rutting season, bulls emit a bugle that is a sign of dominance and a challenge to other bulls. The bugle starts off as a bellow and changes to a shrill scream that can often be heard for miles. Dominance between bulls is determined in rutting contests where elk clash antlers with one another. The most dominant bulls have been known to assemble harems of up to 60 females.

U.S. RANGE

Found on N. & S. Rim in Grand Canyon

INFO

Weight: 600–1,000 pounds

Shoulder Height: 4.5–5 feet

Length: 6–9 feet

Tracks:

MULE DEER

Odocoileus hemionus

Mule deer are the most commonly encountered large mammal in the park. They are frequently seen grazing near the railroad tracks in Grand Canyon Village. Although closely related to white-tailed deer, mule deer are slightly larger and have white tails with a black tip. Mule deer are found predominantly in mountainous areas of the arid Southwest. They are named for their large ears that move independently of each other—like a mule.

Bucks grow antlers that are shed each winter. Although conflict between bucks is infrequent, mild fights sometimes break out. In these fights antlers are enmeshed while each buck tries to force the head of the other down. Injuries are rare, but if the antlers become locked both bucks will be unable to feed and will ultimately die of starvation. Fights between does are much more common. As a result, family groups tend to be spaced widely apart. Young does give birth to one fawn, but older does often give birth to twins. Fawns are able to distinguish their mother from other does through a unique odor produced by glands on the mother's hind legs.

U.S. RANGE

Found on N. & S. Rim in Grand Canyon

INFO

Weight: 150–200 pounds

Shoulder Height: 3–3.5 feet

Length: 5–7 feet

Tracks:

MOUNTAIN LION

Felis concolor

Mountain lions, also known as pumas or cougars, have the most extensive range of any North American mammal—stretching from Canada to Argentina. At one time they inhabited all 48 lower states, but in the late 1800s and early 1900s mountain lions in the United States were hunted to the brink of extinction. Following strict hunting regulations, they have made a steady comeback in some wilderness areas, especially the Four Corners region.

Mountain lions are the largest wildcats in North America. They are quick, efficient killers that can travel up to 25 miles a day in search of prey. A mountain lion will generally stalk animals to within 30 feet before attacking. When they pounce they can leap up to 20 feet in a single bound, killing their victims by inflicting a lethal bite that severs the spinal cord. Mountain lions feed primarily on deer—killing up to one a week. They also feed on elk, coyotes, and big horn sheep.

Mountain lions are almost never seen in the park, but use extreme caution if you do encounter one. Although there has never been an attack in Grand Canyon National Park, they have been known to attack humans elsewhere.

U.S. RANGE

Found in remote areas in Grand Canyon

INFO

Weight: 100–200 pounds

Shoulder Height: 4.5–5 feet

Length: 6–9 feet

Tracks:

RATTLESNAKES

Crotalus scutulatus (below), Crotalus viridis abyssus (right)

There are six species of rattlesnakes in the Grand Canyon, including the Mojave Rattlesnake (above) and Grand Canyon Rattlesnake (right). Rattlers are the only venomous snakes in the canyon, but they are seldom seen above the rim. Although they have poor eyesight, they have a sharp sense of smell and can detect body heat through infrared sensors located on either side of their head. These keen senses are used to detect prey while a rattler lies in wait. When the rattler strikes its victim, it injects a paralyzing venom through sharp fangs. Once the victim is motionless, the rattler swallows it whole. Rattlers, in turn, are preyed upon by such animals as coyotes, eagles, and hawks. Hawks will pluck rattlers from the ground, then drop them repeatedly from the air until the snake is dead.

The inner Grand Canyon is the only place in the world where the Grand Canyon Rattlesnake, a subspecies of the Western Rattlesnake, is found. It evolved over millions of years in the confines of the canyon. The Grand Canyon Rattler is distinguished by its pale, pinkish coloration, and irregular, dark blotches that become paler toward the center.

U.S. RANGE

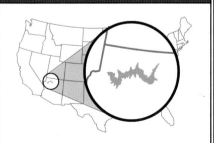

Grand Canyon Rattlesnake

U.S. RANGE

Mojave Rattlesnake

BALD EAGLE

Haliaeetus leucocephalus

Bald eagles range over much of North America, including Alaska and Mexico. At one time there may have been as many as 75,000 bald eagles in the lower 48 states, but by the early 1960s there were fewer than 900. Hunting and the effects of DDT, a pesticide that severely weakened the eggs of birds, brought the bald eagle to the brink of extinction throughout much of its natural range. They were officially listed as endangered in 1967. Since then, the birds have made a remarkable comeback. There are now roughly 70,000 bald eagles in North America, with over half found in Alaska.

Although bald eagles range over a vast territory, most return to nest within 100 miles of where they were raised. Nests are re-used year after year and are added to annually. (Some nests can reach 10 feet across and weigh up to 2,000 pounds.) Young bald eagles do not develop their distinctive white head until their fourth or fifth year. Adult birds have up to 7,000 feathers.

U.S. RANGE

Found throughout the Grand Canyon

INFO

Wingspan: 8 feet

Length: 40 inches

Weight: 14 pounds

Lifespan: 30 years

Population: 70,000

CALIFORNIA CONDOR

Gymnogyps californianus

California condors are the largest and most spectacular birds in the park. Although their historic range once extended from British Columbia to Baja California, by 1982 the worldwide California condor population had plummeted to 22 birds—the result of habitat loss, shootings, and birds feeding on poisonous lead-shot in carcasses left by hunters. With the species at the brink of extinction, the last remaining birds were captured and bred in captivity. In the 1990s condors were reintroduced to central California and the Grand Canyon.

Although captive-bred condors have done remarkably well in the Grand Canyon, it remains to be seen if they can successfully reproduce in the wild. Condor reproduction is a slow process—condors do not reach sexual maturity until six years of age, and an adult pair typically raises only one chick every other year. But there are encouraging signs. In 2003 a condor chick that hatched in the park fledged—the first known occurrence in Arizona in over 100 years.

Condors can be spotted soaring in the thermals above the Grand Canyon. Although they are easily confused with turkey vultures, condors have much larger wingspans and triangular white coloring on the underside of their wings.

U.S. RANGE

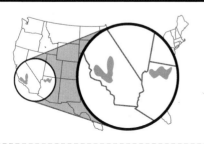

Found throughout the Grand Canyon

INFO

Wingspan: 10 feet

Weight: 20 pounds

Lifespan: 60 years

Southwest population: ~40

Total population: ~200

PEREGRINE FALCON

Falco peregrinus

Peregrine falcons are birds of prey that hunt other birds with deadly accuracy. They have exceptional vision and can spot prey from thousands of feet above. Once a target is selected, peregrines dive bomb it at speeds topping 200 miles per hour. The resulting collision creates an explosion of feathers, and prey that does not die upon impact has its neck broken by the peregrine's specially designed beak. Peregrines are such successful strikers that they were used by British troops to kill Nazi carrier pigeons in World War II.

By the early 1970s, peregrine falcons sat at the brink of extinction. Effects of the pesticide DDT had reduced the total peregrine population to less than 40 pairs. To save the birds, young peregrines were raised in captivity and released in the wild. These programs have been remarkably successful. There are now over 1,650 breeding pairs in the United States and Canada, and in 1999 the peregrine was removed from the endangered species list.

Peregrines nest on the ledges of tall cliffs, making the Grand Canyon an ideal habitat for the birds. As a result, Grand Canyon National Park now has the largest population of peregrines in the Southwest.

U.S. RANGE

Found on tall cliffs in the Grand Canyon

INFO

Wingspan: 41 inches

Length: 16 inches

Weight: 1.6 pounds

Lifespan: 15 years

Population: 3,300

HUMPBACK CHUB

Gila cypha

The humpback chub is the Grand Canyon's most famous native fish. It first appeared 3–5 million years ago in the white water filled canyons of the Colorado River Basin. Because it evolved in swift, muddy waters, the chub has developed some remarkable biological adaptations. Large fins allow it to easily maneuver rapids. Small eyes protect it from silt. And when swift water passes over its pronounced hump, the fish is forced down toward the bottom of the river where the current is less strong, helping it stay put during floods.

The humpback chub once thrived in the Colorado, but they are now on the verge of extinction due to dams, which have significantly lowered water temperatures in the river. Although chubs can survive in cold water, they need warm water to spawn. Today they are forced to spawn in a handful of smaller tributaries. The new Colorado has also allowed non-native species such as trout to invade the chub's natural habitat, competing for resources and feeding on young chub. Although scattered chub populations exist above Lake Powell, the largest remaining chub population—less than 2,000 fish—lives in the Grand Canyon near the junction of the Little Colorado River.

U.S. RANGE

* Historic Range

- -

Found only in Colorado River Basin

INFO

Length: 18 inches

Weight: 2 pounds

Color: Green/silver/white

Lifespan: 30+ years

RAINBOW TROUT

Oncorhynchus mykiss

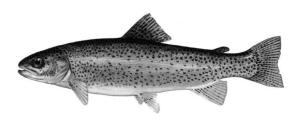

Rainbow trout are one of the world's most prized sport fish. They have an olive/bluish back and a characteristic pink band running down their sides. Although they are native to rivers in the western United States, rainbow trout are extremely adaptable. Over the past century they have been transplanted to rivers in Africa, Japan, Southeast Asia, South America, Europe, Australia, and New Zealand.

Rainbow trout were introduced to the Colorado River just north of the Grand Canyon following the completion of Glen Canyon Dam in 1964. The cool, clear waters released from the bottom of the dam created an ideal trout habitat. After it was stocked it became a world-famous fishery, but some of the trout have found their way downstream to the confluence of the Colorado River and the Little Colorado River—a vital spawning ground for native fish. To prevent the trout from feeding on young native fish, federal employees have recently instituted an aggressive trout removal policy. Trout are shocked with electro-fishing gear, captured, and euthanized. The carcasses are then given to local Indians for use as fertilizer.

U.S. RANGE

Found in rivers throughout the U.S.

INFO

Length: 10–40 inches

Weight: up to 10 pounds

Color: Olive/pink/silver

Lifespan: 6 years

GRAND CANYON
HISTORY

HUMANS FIRST SET eyes on the Grand Canyon around 10,000 years ago, when primitive hunters and gatherers first arrived in Arizona. Little is known about these prehistoric people, but small artifacts found in the backs of caves confirm their existence in the Grand Canyon. Among the artifacts discovered were spear points and small split twig figurines (below) twisted into the shapes of animals. Some of the figurines were pierced with tiny spears made of agave thorns, leaving little doubt that hunting played an important role in the lives of these early settlers.

What ultimately happened to these people is unclear. While they may have abandoned the Grand Canyon, it's just as likely that they stayed. In either case, a new culture called the Ancestral Puebloans (Anasazi) appeared several thousand years later. The Ancestral Puebloans occupied the Four Corners region from roughly A.D. 0 to 1200. For over a thousand years they flourished in the Grand Canyon, which marked the westernmost range of their territory.

Archaeologists have subdivided the Ancestral Puebloans into two distinct groups. The first group, the Basketmakers, lived from A.D. 0 to 700. Named for their exceptional skill at basketry, they wove plant fibers into beautiful baskets and sandals. The early Basketmakers were hunters and gatherers, constantly on the move in search of food. As time passed, however, they discovered agriculture, which allowed them to settle down in one place. They lived in caves or under overhanging cliffs, and grew beans, corn, and squash nearby.

Farming was the Basketmakers' main source of food, but they also hunted animals with spears. This provided them with food and the raw materials for clothing. In the winter the Basketmakers wore robes made of deer skin, rabbit skin, or turkey feathers. In the summer they wore loin clothes and skirts woven from plant fibers. Jewelry was made from seashells imported from the Pacific Coast, and live parrots were imported from Mexico. The Basketmakers kept dogs as pets, smoked tobacco from pipes, and played music on six-hole flutes. By A.D. 600 they had also learned to make pottery, but more striking cultural advances were yet to come.

Around A.D. 700 the Basketmakers discovered the bow and arrow. This new weapon allowed them to hunt more food in less time, and with more free time on their hands they continued to advance. Soon they were using stone masonry to build impressive stone villages under the awnings of cliffs. A number of these dwellings, such as Canyon de Chelly in northeast Arizona and Chaco Canyon in New Mexico, are some of the most spectacular archaeological landmarks in America.

As Ancestral Puebloan living quarters advanced, so did the rules governing their society. Customs and social codes became highly developed. Some villages may have operated like independent city-states. These social advances were so profound that archaeologists have subdivided the later Ancestral Puebloans into a second cultural group: the Pueblo Anasazi.

The Pueblo Anasazi continued to advance, building irrigation ditches near fertile areas and storing excess crops in granaries (stone storage compartments). The granaries were so well constructed that many remain intact to this day. Artistic achievements also blossomed during this time. Cotton was spun and woven into beautiful clothes, and dwellings were covered with murals and pictographs. Elaborate costumes, decorated with turquoise and tiny bells, were used in religious ceremonies.

By the 1100s the Ancestral Puebloans were flourishing in the Grand Canyon. They occupied thousands of sites both above and below the rim, and were considered some of the most advanced Indians north of Mexico. But at the height of their prosperity, the Ancestral Puebloans abandoned their settlements and disappeared from the Grand Canyon.

Modern archaeologists are at a loss to explain what caused the Ancestral Puebloans to leave. Theories abound, but little is actually known. Some archaeologists believe the Ancestral Puebloans fell victim to a massive drought. Others blame their demise on a depletion of natural resources. Still others think that there may have been a great war between neighboring tribes. Whatever the case, after abandoning their settlements in the Grand Canyon, many Ancestral Puebloans moved south and merged with the Hopi and Zuni tribes.

Shortly after the Ancestral Puebloan departure the region saw a new wave of human settlement. Within a few centuries modern tribes such as the Havasupai, Hualapai, Southern Paiute, Hopi. and Navajo had settled the surrounding territory.

Ancestral Puebloan pottery

THE MYSTERY
— *of the* —
ANCESTRAL PUEBLOANS

THE MASS EXODUS of the Ancestral Puebloans from the Grand Canyon is one of the Southwest's greatest archaeological mysteries. Why would a culture at the height of its prosperity—by many accounts the most advanced culture north of Mexico—suddenly abandon its settlements?

For decades the accepted theory was that the Ancestral Puebloans fell victim to a massive drought. Scientists have long known that the Southwest experienced a period of decreased rainfall in the late 1200s, but modern evidence suggests that this so-called Great Drought would not have been enough to cause a complete cultural collapse. Besides, they had survived many droughts in the past. Why should this one be any different? It also appears that the Ancestral Puebloans started to abandon their settlements prior to the drought.

Ancestral
Puebloan
Sandal

Some archaeologists believe that the Ancestral Puebloan abandonment was triggered by a depletion of the region's scarce natural resources due to overpopulation. Chronic shortages of plants and animals would have led to social and political upheaval—and possibly even war. Archaeologists are quick to point out that many Ancestral Puebloan structures built near the end appear to be defensive in nature.

But if there was a war, why didn't the winners stay to enjoy the spoils? Some scholars have recently suggested that it wasn't war that brought down the Ancestral Puebloans, but a religious collapse. Religion and daily life were one and the same to Ancestral Puebloans, and a collapse of one would have inevitably led to a collapse of the other. Faced with failing crops, chronic shortages, and rain dances that no longer worked, the Ancestral Puebloans may have lost faith in their prevailing religion. At the same time, the Hopi's new Katsina religion was gaining momentum to the south. With its colored masks and lurid dances, the Katsina religion could have lured the Ancestral Puebloans away from their homeland.

While these theories offer possible explanations, many unanswered questions remain. Until new evidence comes to light, the Ancestral Puebloans' abandonment will continue to be one of the Grand Canyon's best-kept secrets.

northern arizona
TRIBES

THE HOPI

The Hopi are one of the oldest cultures in the region, having lived in northeast Arizona for over a thousand years. Oraibi, a Hopi village located about 80 miles east of the Grand Canyon, was settled over 800 years ago, making it the oldest continuously inhabited town in the United States.

The Grand Canyon is a deeply symbolic place for the Hopi. They believe that both people and animals emerged from the Grand Canyon at a place called the *Sipaapuni*, a mineral spring located near the junction of the Colorado and Little Colorado Rivers.

The Hopi religion revolves around *Katsinas*, spirit beings who live in the San Francisco Mountains north of Flagstaff. Katsinas are believed to visit Hopi villages for a few months each year, performing good deeds, punishing criminals, and (most importantly) bringing rain. The Hopi craft hundreds of brightly painted wooden dolls, called *Tihu*, to represent different Katsinas. Tihu—also called Katsina or Kachina Dolls—were traditionally carved from a single piece of cottonwood root, and given to children to teach them about the different Katsinas.

SOUTHERN PAIUTE

The Southern Paiute settled the plateau country north of the Grand Canyon around A.D. 1300. Because resources in the region were limited, they found it easier to exist in small bands rather than as large groups governed by complex social structures. Each band had an individual leader who served the role of a tribal advisor. The leader was an elderly man who had spent a lifetime studying the landscape, and he imparted his knowledge of plants and animals to others.

The Southern Paiute hunted deer and small game on the Kaibab Plateau that encompasses much of the North Rim. *Kaibab* is derived from a Paiute word meaning "Mountain Lying Down." While the men hunted, the women gathered plants. Eventually the Southern Paiute adopted agriculture from the Hopi and Navajo.

THE PAI

Although recorded as two separate tribes by early American explorers, the Havasupai and Hualapai consider themselves members of the same Pai culture. The Havasupai have been living in the deep canyons of the western Grand Canyon for over 700 years. Their neighbors, the Hualapai, have occupied the South Rim's western plateaus for roughly the same period of time.

The Hualapai, "Pine Tree People," spent most of their time in the forests plateaus above the Grand Canyon. In the summer they would sometimes gather plants in the rugged side canyons that drop down from the South Rim.

The Havasupai, "People of the Blue-Green Water," take their name from the beautiful turquoise pools and waterfalls in Havasu Canyon (p.318). Because they had access to constant water, the Havasupai grew more food than any other tribe in the region. Havasu Creek, one of the most dependable water sources in the Grand Canyon, helped the Havasupai weather even the greatest droughts.

THE NAVAJO

The Navajo were one of the last tribes to settle the Grand Canyon region. They arrived from northwest Canada sometime between 500 and 1000 years ago, settling just east of the Grand Canyon. But when they reached the desert they were forced to adopt a new way of life. Unable to survive on their own, they raided the villages of previously settled tribes. Eventually they learned agriculture from their neighbors.

Traditional Navajo homes are called *hogans*, one-room buildings built out of logs and tree branches. The doorway to a hogan always faces east so the Navajo can start each day by greeting the light of the rising sun. The Navajo believe that humans must live in harmony with nature, achieving a sense of place called *hozho*. They refer to themselves *Dine*, "The People."

In the 1600s the Spanish introduced sheep to the Navajo. Before long, Navajo culture revolved around sheep herding. Sheep meat soon replaced deer meat as the primary source of protein in the Navajo diet, and sheep wool was woven into beautiful rugs with colorful designs. Navajo legend speaks of two animal beings, Spider Man and Spider Woman, who taught the Navajo how to build looms and weave.

Coronado Expedition

A FABLED CITY OF GOLD

LESS THAN 30 years after Columbus discovered North America, Spanish conquistador Hernan Cortez defeated the Aztecs in Mexico. At the time Spain was the most powerful country in the world. Hoping to expand its empire both at home and abroad, Spain pursued an aggressive policy of empire building. But empire building is an expensive proposition, and despite the vast wealth plundered from the Aztecs, Spain was soon desperate for additional funds.

Then, several years after the fall of the Aztec, a Spanish sailing expedition shipwrecked off the Texas coast. The wreck's four survivors spent the next seven years wandering the desert. When they returned to Mexico they told stories of a fabulous city of gold located somewhere in the American Southwest. This city, soon referred to as the Seven Cities of Cibola, quickly captured the imagination of the impoverished Spanish crown.

In 1540 Spanish authorities assembled a military expedition to locate the Seven Cities of Cibola. Led by a charismatic 29-year-old named Francisco Vasquez de Coronado, the expedition consisted of 300 Spanish men, several hundred Indians, and thousands of cattle, sheep, and goats. Five months later the expedition reached the spot where the Seven Cities were rumored to be located. All the Spaniards found was a small Indian village built out of stone and mud.

Coronado was dejected, but the Indians he encountered told him of a larger group of seven cities to the west. Coronado immediately dispatched his lieutenant, Don Pedro de Tovar, to investigate these claims. Tovar reported back that he had failed to locate the Seven Cites of Cibola, but he had learned of mighty river to the west. Hoping this river was the gateway to Cibola, Coronado dispatched another search party under the command of Garcia Lopez de Cardenas.

After three weeks of travel Cardenas' party reached the South Rim of the Grand Canyon. They were the first white men to set eyes on the Grand Canyon, but they were hardly impressed by what they saw. From their vantage point on the South Rim—believed to be somewhere between Moran Point and Desert View—the Spaniards estimated the Colorado River to be just six feet wide (the average width of the Colorado in the Grand Canyon is closer to 300 feet). Although their Hopi guides insisted that the river was much larger, the Spaniards refused to believe them. They had never encountered a natural structure of this scale, and were unable to comprehend its true dimensions

For three days the Spaniards tried to find a route to the river. One group of soldiers made it a third of the way down, but they were unable to descend any further. Once back they reported that rocks that appeared no more than a few feet high from the rim were actually taller than the 185-foot tower of Seville in Spain. Suddenly comprehending the true size of the Grand Canyon, Cardenas turned his men around. Although Coronado's expedition continued to search throughout the Southwest for the Seven Cities of Cibola, they were never found.

THE SECOND SPANISH WAVE

IN THE DECADES following Coronado's failed expedition, Spain once again ignored the Southwest. No colonization attempts were made until 1598, when Jaun de Onate founded Santa Fe, New Mexico. Thirty years later Spanish missionaries established a handful of missions near Hopi towns.

The Hopi's initial reaction to the missions was one of deep resentment. They had no interest in changing their religious beliefs, and did not want the Spanish interfering in their daily lives. By 1680 Indian mistrust reached a breaking point. In that year leaders from several tribes met in secret to plan a coordinated revolt against the Spanish. The Pueblo Revolt, as it was later called, was a resounding success. It drove out the Spanish and allowed the Indians to regain complete control of their territories.

But the Indians' sense of sovereignty did not last long. Twelve years after the Pueblo Revolt, a more powerful Spanish army marched north to reconquer the Southwest. In response to the new threat the Hopi retreated to villages on the tops of tall mesas, which could be easily defended from above. Before long, Hopi mesas had become a favored destination for many Indians seeking refuge from the Spanish.

While the Hopi and the Navajo fought the Spanish to the east of the Grand Canyon, Indians living in the remote western Grand Canyon remained relatively undisturbed. Still, a handful of rugged Spanish explorers managed to pass through.

In 1776 a Franciscan missionary named Tomas Garces attempted to blaze a trail between Spanish missions in California and the Rio Grande. His journey led him up the Colorado River into the western Grand Canyon. When he encountered Havasupai Indians they invited him to stay for five days of feasting, after which Garces set out to visit the Hopi villages to the east. But the Hopi were deeply suspicious of the Spanish. They refused to feed Garces or even accept his gifts. Taking the hint, Garces returned to Havasu Canyon where he was greeted with another multiday feast.

Not long after Garces journey another Spanish expedition, the Dominguez-Escalante party, left New Mexico to find a northern route to the Pacific Coast. They had planned on crossing the Sierra Nevada Mountains before winter, but the priests in their party spent so much time preaching along the way that they arrived after the deep winter snows had set in. Forced to abandon their mission, the Spaniards headed south. At one point they crossed the Colorado near the present site of Lees Ferry, becoming the third and final Spanish expedition to visit the Grand Canyon.

Although the Spanish had relatively little contact with many of the Indians living near the Grand Canyon, their indirect presence had a huge impact on Indian culture. The Spanish introduced horses, cattle, and sheep to North America—animals that would come to define many Southwestern tribes. The Spanish also introduced new fruits such as peaches, melons, and figs. But along with these positive influences came many deadly diseases such as smallpox, which had a devastating impact on Indians throughout the Southwest.

Indian Pueblo

AMERICAN EXPLORERS

I N 1821 MEXICO gained independence from Spain and acquired much of the American Southwest. But despite the region's new owner, little changed in terms of its day-to-day use. Like the Spanish before them Mexico generally avoided the Southwest. Indians living near the Grand Canyon remained relatively undisturbed, but a new threat was looming on the eastern horizon.

Following the Louisiana Purchase, American beaver trappers began fanning out across the West. Before long they were scouring the streams that tumbled down from the Rockies and exploring the Four Corners region. Even the Grand Canyon was avoided as a destination. Although beavers live at the bottom of the Grand Canyon, reaching them proved too arduous a task.

Not that some trappers didn't try. In 1826 a trapping party led by Ewing Young traveled up the Colorado River on foot to become the first Americans to set eyes on the Grand Canyon. Their journey was a miserable one. At one point the men plodded through 18 inches of snow and ate bark to fend off starvation. Not surprisingly, they found little to like about the region. As one of the trappers, James Pattie, remembered, "We arrived where the river emerges from these horrid mountains, which so cage it up, as to deprive all human beings of the ability to descend to its banks, and make use of its waters."

Such descriptions did little to encourage further exploration. With its extreme climate, physically challenging terrain, and striking lack of water, the Four Corners region was a terrible place to settle, which was precisely why Mormon leader Brigham Young decided to settle there.

THE EXPLORER

I N 1857 THE War Department selected a novice Lieutenant named Joseph Christmas Ives to lead an expedition to explore the lower reaches of the Colorado River. Unfortunately, his 50-foot sternwheeler, *The Explorer*, was poorly designed to handle the rapids, shallows, and sand bars of the Colorado. The boat ran aground countless times and the crew was often forced to unload and tow it by hand. After two months of slow progress, *The Explorer* struck a submerged boulder near the present site of Hoover Dam. The men were tossed overboard and the ship was wrecked beyond repair. Ives declared they had reached the furthest point of navigation on the river.

Not only was Ives' declaration inaccurate, he had already been proven wrong. Several weeks earlier, a man named George Johnson, incensed at being passed over to lead the historic expedition, had steamed his own boat up Black Canyon.

Although Ives' expedition produced several fine maps of the region, much of the Colorado remained as mysterious as ever. Before leaving, Ives concluded his journey with the unfortunate remark: "The region is, of course, altogether valueless. It can be approached only from the south, and after entering it there is nothing to do but leave. Ours has been the first, and will doubtless be the last, party of whites to visit this profitless locality."

Today, the Grand Canyon, Hoover Dam, and nearby Las Vegas attract over 40 million visitors a year.

Fleeing religious persecution in Illinois, Young led his followers to the Great Salt Lake area in 1847. The harsh landscape offered the perfect refuge for the Mormons; a place where they could practice their religion in peace. Over time their settlements would spread south, representing the first significant white presence anywhere near the Grand Canyon. But even the Mormons weren't crazy enough to explore the interior of the Grand Canyon. That job would fall to a 34-year-old geology professor named John Wesley Powell.

JOHN WESLEY POWELL

FOLLOWING THE CONCLUSION of the Mexican War in 1848, the United States acquired the vast chunk of land that would one day make up California, Nevada, Arizona, Utah, Colorado, and New Mexico. But even in the 1860s, maps of the United States had a single word splashed across the Grand Canyon region: UNEXPLORED. Most men, even the heroically rugged trappers who had opened up the West, took one look at these maps and decided to stay away. But one man took a look at these maps and saw an opportunity for everlasting fame.

John Wesley Powell was probably the least likely man in America to conquer the Colorado River in the Grand Canyon. A one-armed college professor with virtually no whitewater experience, Powell was a case study in everything that wasn't needed to successfully navigate the Colorado. At 5 feet six inches he hardly cut an imposing figure. But what Powell lacked in physical stature, he more than made up for in personal ambition.

In 1868 Powell decided to organize an expedition to explore the Colorado River and its canyons. He traveled to Washington, D.C. to raise money for the trip, but with the federal treasury still reeling from the Civil War, government money was hard to come by. He was offered some military rations, however, which he gladly accepted.

HERO or LIAR?

IN 1867, two years before Powell's expedition, a raft was pulled from the Colorado River just below the Grand Canyon. On board was a starving, sunburned, half-naked man named James White (right). He proceeded to tell a story so amazing that it is still disputed to this day. According to White, he had spent the previous two weeks floating through the Grand Canyon lashed to a raft, making him the first man to successfully run the Grand Canyon. Most modern scholars dispute White's story, based primarily on the fact that it's so hard to believe. But supposing it is true, White's journey would have been one of the most remarkable whitewater adventures of all time

With persistence, Powell managed to scrape together funding from a variety of private institutions.

His next step was to assemble a crew. The job offered no pay, harsh living conditions, and life-threatening risks. Not surprisingly, the men who accepted these terms were reckless, crazy, or a little of both. Most were trappers and mountain men eager for adventure and excitement. But to Powell, the journey was primarily a scientific expedition. "The object," he wrote, " is to make collections in geology, natural history, antiquities, and ethnology."

Powell's expedition launched their four boats on May 24, 1869 from Green River City, Wyoming. Their starting point was 6,100 feet above sea level. Their destination—the Grand Wash Cliffs, near present-day Lake Mead—lay at an elevation of 1,300 feet. How the river got there was anybody's guess.

For the first week of their journey the men floated peacefully down the Green River. The one-armed Powell, unable to row, sat perched on a chair tied to his boat. At first the slow current bored the men, but soon the river started to intensify. As they continued downstream the rapids became more frequent and fierce. Then, on June 9, one of their boats slipped into a rapid before they had a chance to scout it. The boat smashed against a rock and splintered into pieces. Although the three men onboard managed to swim to safety, a third of the expedition's supplies were lost.

Following Disaster Falls (as Powell later named it) a nervous energy settled over the crew. They were only two weeks into their journey and they had already lost one

rescue by
UNDERWEAR!

IN DESOLATION Canyon, Powell and a crew member named George Bradley set out to climb the steep cliffs above the river. As the one-armed Powell neared the top he became stranded on the edge of a cliff. "Standing on my toes my muscles began to tremble," he wrote. "If I lose my hold I shall fall to the bottom." Powell called to Bradley, who quickly appeared on a ledge above. With time running out, Bradley stripped off his long johns and lowered them to Powell. They dangled behind Powell just out of reach. There was only one option. Powell took a deep breath, leaned back into space, and grabbed for the long johns with his one good hand. Catching a pant leg he held on for dear life while Bradley hauled him up to safety.

Wreck at Disaster Falls

Powell Expedition boats

of their boats. What would happen if they lost another? The rapids were only growing worse, and soon they would be hundreds of miles from civilization.

Determined, the men carried on. For the next two months they followed the Green River as it passed through Wyoming and Utah, running rapids whenever they could but spending most of the time lining or portaging. Lining involved guiding the boats downstream as the men held on to ropes from the shore. It was excruciating work. The ropes burned the men's hands and they were constantly slipping on wet rocks. The alternative was portaging. It entailed carrying the boats—and several thousand pounds of supplies—past the rapid on shore.

By the time the expedition reached the confluence of the Green and the Grand (the official start of the Colorado) supplies were running low. They were down to several pounds of spoiled bacon, a few sacks of flour, and some dried apples. The men tried to supplement their diet by hunting, but game in the region was scarce. Before long, the constant hunger and backbreaking days were taking a serious toll on the group's morale.

On August 4 the expedition reached the beginning of the Grand Canyon. Powell was spellbound by the variety of rocks he saw. The highly polished limestone looked like marble, and Powell named this stretch Marble Canyon. As they continued through Marble Canyon the cliffs rose up thousands of feet on either side. The scale of the canyon was breathtaking. "We are three quarters of a mile in the depths of the Earth," Powell wrote, "and the great river shrinks into insignificance, as it dashes its angry waves against the walls and cliffs, that rise to the world above; they are but puny ripples, and we are but pygmies."

While Powell marveled at the natural spectacle, many of his crew felt confined. The canyon was like a prison to them. Daytime highs topped 100°F and the rapids were frequent and fierce. Many began to openly regret their decision to come.

Continuing on, the men twisted deep in the heart of the Grand Canyon. They were now fighting off rapids the size of three-story buildings. Making matters worse, they had no idea what to expect around each bend. Rumors existed of giant waterfalls in the Grand Canyon. If these rumors proved true, the expedition would find itself trapped at the bottom of a mile deep chasm. Physically and mentally, the men were starting to unwind. They were now down to starvation rations, and the threat of death was very real.

On August 27 a man named Oramel Howland took Powell aside. Powell knew what was coming. The men were camped above their worst rapid yet, and many in the group doubted they could run it and survive. Howland told Powell that he and two others were abandoning the expedition. They would take their chances climbing out of the canyon, even though that decision carried equally lethal implications.

Powell respected their decision, but he was convinced the rapid could be run. And according to his calculations, they were no more than 50 miles from the end of their journey. He spent all night trying to convince the men not to leave, but they had seen enough. The three men left the following morning. They were never seen again. Most people believe they were killed by Indians, but no one knows for sure.

Concentrating on the matter at hand, Powell studied the rapid. The river was hemmed in by steep cliffs, so there was no possibility of portaging. And other than

a small section at the top of the rapid, lining was also out of the question. With a slimmed down crew the men abandoned one of the boats. They lined the remaining two boats as far as they could and swooped down into the rapid.

The first boat rushed down the steep face of a wave and was swamped with water. The men pulled for their lives. Soon the waves, "grew too large to do anything but hold on to the boats." The boats tossed and turned and swirled about, but somehow they managed to stay upright. Before the men knew it, the rapid was behind them. Both boats had survived.

Two days later Powell's expedition reached the end of its journey. As they approached the confluence of the Colorado and the Virgin River, the men spotted several Mormons fishing in the river. The Mormons had been posted there for weeks, under orders from Brigham Young to keep their eyes out "for any fragments or relics of [Powell's] party that might drift down the stream." They were stunned to see Powell and his men alive.

The skeletal river runners were overwhelmed with joy. The Mormons immediately cooked them a meal, and as one of the crew remembered, "we laid our dignified manners aside and assumed the manner of so many hogs. Ate as long as we could and went to sleep to wake up hungry." After 99 days on the river, their voyage was over.

Powell's historic journey seems almost hallucinatory today. River guides who have spent decades rowing the modern, regulated Colorado simply shake their heads in awe when they try to comprehend what Powell accomplished. His under supplied, ragtag collection of mountain men conquered the wildest river in North America. Today, their journey is often referred to the last great expedition of the American West.

John Wesley Powell
1834–1902

John Wesley Powell grew up the son of a poor itinerant preacher. As a child, his family moved throughout the Midwest, never staying in one place very long. Even as a young man Powell was constantly on the move. Although he enrolled in several different colleges, he never stayed around long enough to graduate from any of them.

When the Civil War broke out, Powell enlisted on the Union side. He made Lieutenant within his first two months, but was shot in his right arm at the battle of Shiloh. It was an injury that required amputation. Refusing to be kept out of the fight, the one armed Powell returned to action several months later and accompanied General Sherman on his conquest of Georgia.

Following the war, Powell underwent an operation to ease the constant pain in his amputated arm. The operation failed, and for the rest of his life Powell was plagued with chronic pain from the raw nerve endings at the end of his stump. Not one to dwell on personal misfortune, Powell simply looked to the future as he tried to figure out what to do with his life. "You are a maimed man," his father told him, "Settle down at teaching. It is a noble profession. Get this nonsense of science and adventure out of your mind."

Powell tried to settle down at teaching, but the lure of the West proved too powerful. As a geologist he led research trips to the headwaters of the Colorado and Green Rivers—two rivers whose waters ultimately flow through the Grand Canyon. It was there that Powell developed an obsession with the Southwest. Powell the geologist was convinced that the canyons of the Colorado would give "the best geological section on the continent." Powell the adventurer desperately wanted to be the first to conquer the final frontier of the United States.

And conquer it he did. Following his Grand Canyon expedition Powell achieved international fame. On the lecture circuit he spoke to packed houses and stayed in the finest hotels. Later, he used his influence to help found the Bureau of American Ethnology and the U.S. Geological Survey.

Powell died in 1902. Shortly before his death, he made an unusual bet with his friend W.J. McGee, the president of the National Geographic Society. Although he was physically smaller than McGee, Powell was convinced that his brain was larger. To settle the dispute, the men left instructions to have their brains weighed following their deaths. At 1,488 grams, Powell's brain was 5 percent heavier. Today it rests in a jar at the Smithsonian Institute.

grand canyon PIONEERS

JOHN HANCE

JOHN HANCE was the first permanent white settler in the Grand Canyon. He came here on a prospecting trip in 1881 and immediately fell in love with the scenery. Two years later, he built a log cabin east of Grandview Point and started renting out rooms to guests.

Hance is fondly remembered as the Grand Canyon's premier storyteller, but his stories rarely contained a shred of truth. He took great pleasure in spinning tall tales with a deadpan delivery until his hapless listeners realized they'd been had.

One of his favorite stories involved the time the Grand Canyon filled with clouds. According to Hance, he walked across the clouds on snowshoes, but became stranded on a pinnacle when the clouds started to clear. Another time he jumped across the entire canyon on horseback. Hance had hundreds of stories in his repertoire, and he never told the same story twice in exactly the same way.

As Hance once confided to a friend, "I've got to tell stories to them people for their money; and if I don't tell it to them, who will? I can make these tenderfeet believe that a frog eats boiled eggs; and I'm going to do it; and I'm going to make 'em believe that he carries it a mile to find a rock to crack it on."

The tenderfeet loved it. According to one early visitor, "Anyone who comes to the Grand Canyon and fails to meet John Hance will miss half the show." In 1906 he was offered free room and board at the Bright Angel Lodge in exchange for just hanging out with the guests and being himself.

JOHN D. LEE

B EFORE HE was banished to the Grand Canyon by Brigham Young, John D. Lee had been a prosperous Mormon living in southern Utah with his 19 wives. But in 1857 Lee participated in the Mountain Meadow Massacre, in which a group of Mormons slaughtered a wagon train of 120 pioneers on their way to California. In a blatant cover up, the Mormon Church placed the blame solely on Lee's shoulders. With the law at his back, Lee fled to the Grand Canyon.

Lee arrived at a place along the Colorado River just south of present-day Lake Powell. There he established Lees Ferry. It was the only viable river crossing for hundreds of miles. But being a wanted man and owning one of the only ferry crossings for hundreds of miles turned out to be a dangerous combination. In 1874 the law finally caught up with Lee, and he was tried and executed. He was survived by his 53 children.

BILL BASS

B ILL BASS moved to Williams, Arizona from New Jersey in 1883. Several years later, curiosity and prospecting brought him to the South Rim. He would spend the next 41 years of his life there.

Bass came to the Grand Canyon to prospect, but soon turned to tourism as his main source of income. Before long he had built a crude tent camp along the rim that he called Bass Camp. In a shrewd marketing maneuver, he promoted Bass Camp through home-made lantern slides that were displayed throughout the country.

In 1894 Bass guided a young woman named Ada Diefendorf to the beautiful waterfalls in Havasu Canyon. The two were married a short while later, and Ada became the first white woman to raise a family on the rim of the Grand Canyon. It was hardly an easy life. In addition to household duties such as cooking and cleaning, Ada had to wrangle horses, care for livestock, and hike three days to do laundry in the Colorado River.

In 1926, at the age of 77, Bass sold his claims to the land and retired to Wickenburg, Arizona. By the time he left, he had built more roads and inner-canyon trails than any other individual in Grand Canyon history.

EARLY SETTLERS

P OWELL'S JOURNEY INAUGURATED a wave of expeditions to map and explore the Grand Canyon. Leading this charge was John Wesley Powell himself. Shortly after his historic near-death, near-mutiny expedition, Powell announced plans to lead a second trip down the Colorado. Many of his scientific notes had been lost on the first journey, and he was determined to fill in the blanks. This time, however, he would break his trip into stages with supply points along the way, significantly reducing the risks involved. And so, in 1871, the indefatigable Powell conquered the Colorado again.

Between river trips Powell conducted scientific expeditions along the rim. But these excursions were only temporary. The region as a whole remained largely un-inhabited. Then, following the arrival of the railroad in northern Arizona in the early 1880s, a handful of drifters started taking up permanent residence along the South Rim.

Most of these early settlers were miners who envisioned vast mineral potential in the Grand Canyon's exposed rocks. Although a number of rich mining sites were located, the costs of excavation soon proved prohibitively expensive. Ore had to be packed out on burros, water was scarce, and the closest railroad lay two days away. Mining the Grand Canyon, it tuned out, was an extremely unprofitable endeavor. But just as that realization started to sink in, miners discovered another source of revenue: tourists.

Starting in the mid-1880s, people began arriving at the Grand Canyon for no other reason than to visit, relax, and take in the views. This was a strikingly new concept. For hundreds of years the Grand Canyon had been avoided—even detested—as a destination. Now, people thought it was beautiful. It was an idea that would turn out to be highly contagious.

The first tourists arrived at the South Rim in 1884. They stayed in makeshift accommodations provided by miners. Most visitors arrived by stagecoach from the nearby towns of Flagstaff, Williams, and Ash Fork, but the journey was a rugged one. The dirt roads were filled with potholes, and the trip sometimes required at least two days of bone-jarring travel.

It wasn't long before people began looking for a better form of transportation to the rim. In 1885 Bill Bass brought a railroad agent to his lodge to try to convince him of the potential of a spur line to the Grand Canyon. The agent was not impressed. "No one," he wrote to his superiors, "would go that far only to see a hole in the ground."

It would take over a decade for the railroads to realize their mistake. When they finally did, the previously isolated Grand Canyon would find itself linked directly to the modern world, and visitors would arrive by the thousands.

Grand Canyon Railroad

THE RAILROAD ARRIVES

MINERS AT THE rim weren't the only ones interested in a railroad to the Grand Canyon. The nearby towns of Flagstaff and Williams also realized the benefits that a railroad would bring—namely increased tourist dollars—and both towns were soon engaged in a feverish competition to build one. Flagstaff envisioned a railroad supported by tourism. The town's leading citizens pitched their idea to a number of established railroad companies, but as Bill Bass had already discovered, the railroads failed to grasp the tourist potential of the Grand Canyon.

Williams took a different approach. It appealed to the mining companies who needed a cheap way to haul ore from mines located just south of the canyon. Mining operations would be the driving force of the new railroad, with tourists providing additional revenue. It was a shrewd pitch, and in 1897 the Santa Fe and Grand Canyon Railway Company was incorporated to build a railroad connecting Williams to the South Rim.

Four years later, the Santa Fe Railroad reached Grand Canyon Village. By that time the mines that had spearheaded its creation had already shut down. But that didn't matter. For $3.95 passengers could now enjoy a smooth, four-hour ride to the South Rim (as opposed to the $20, bouncing, all-day stage ride that was previously the only option). The result was predictable. Tourism boomed.

Visitors arrived by the thousands. The railroad flourished and before long land near Grand Canyon Village had become one of the most desirable commodities in the region. A few cunning locals began staking bogus mining claims along the South Rim, giving them the questionable right to develop the land. Although the practice was ultimately ruled illegal, a few citizens—most notably Ralph Cameron (p.100)—became very rich off the scheme.

Bogus mining claims aside, the Santa Fe Railroad still owned most of the land surrounding its tracks, making it the dominant player in the local real estate game. To accommodate the flood of new visitors, it built an extravagant new hotel—the El Tovar—in Grand Canyon Village in 1905. Early settlers who had built hotels away from Grand Canyon Village soon found it hard to compete. Within a decade, most locally owned hotels had shut down.

Life on the rim was changing fast. Just three months after the first train pulled into the South Rim depot, the first automobile arrived. Its driver had departed from Flagstaff several days earlier amid much fanfare, but the car broke down soon after it left. Several days later the automobile arrived at the South Rim pulled by a team of mules. Still, the trip was hardly a bad omen. Within two and a half decades automobiles would become the most popular form of transportation to the Grand Canyon, ultimately forcing the railroad out of business.

While the South Rim was buzzing with tourist activity, the North Rim remained as isolated as ever. Settlement was scarce, and there were no railroads for over a hundred miles. Because of its extreme isolation, the Arizona Strip—the narrow stretch of land between the North Rim and Utah—was a lawless area that attracted a strange mix of cattle thieves, renegades, and Mormons who continued to practice polygamy (some Mormons in the Arizona Strip continue to practice polygamy to this day). Although Utah tried several times to annex the Arizona Strip, citing Arizona's poor law enforcement as a primary concern, Arizona was able to retain control of the land.

Because of its remote location, the North Rim was filled with wild game, a fact soon that attracted hunting parties. Sport hunting on the North Rim got off to a rocky start in 1892 when a man named John Young came up with the idea of building a hunting lodge that would cater to British aristocrats. Young contacted Buffalo Bill Cody, who was performing in England at the time, and convinced him to round up a group of potential British investors. The eager Britons arrived at the North Rim later that year. They took one look around and hightailed it back to England.

American hunters, on the other hand, were more than happy to venture to the North Rim, and sport hunting flourished. In 1906 Congress established the Grand Canyon Game Reserve, which included much of the North Rim. A few years later ex-President Theodore Roosevelt visited the North Rim on a hunting trip. Starting from the South Rim, he descended the Bright Angel trail and crossed the river via a cable system that shuttled passengers back and forth across the river in a large metal cage. Halfway across the river one of the cables snapped. The cage jolted, but it was still in working order. Once the President was safely across, he is said to have remarked, "Let's do it again!"

High-profile visits like these focused even greater attention on the Grand Canyon. It soon became clear that the region was not just a fly-by-night tourist destination, but a major national landmark. Many felt that it deserved to be recognized as such. Before long, the wheels were in motion to create Grand Canyon National Park.

the LION HUNTER

IN 1906 James "Uncle Jim" Owens (left) was appointed manager of the newly established Grand Canyon Game Reserve. Game was now legally protected in the Grand Canyon, but the legal definition of game did not apply to predators such as bobcats and mountain lions. In fact, these animals were aggressively hunted to protect other, less threatening game. During his time on the North Rim, Uncle Jim claimed to have shot over 1,200 mountain lions. Others put that number closer to 550. Regardless, the walls of his cabin were covered with mountain lion claws and a sign outside advertised, "Lions Caught to Order, Reasonable Rates." At one point the famous western novelist Zane Grey accompanied Uncle Jim on a hunting trip. He later chronicled his adventure in the book *Roping Lions in the Grand Canyon*. It wasn't until several decades later that predator hunting was finally banned in the Grand Canyon.

the south rim
SWINDLER

O F ALL THE real estate swindlers who came to the Grand Canyon, none was more successful than Ralph Cameron (left). Shortly after the arrival of the railroad, Cameron began staking mining claims along the South Rim. Before long he had staked over 13,000 acres. But Cameron had little interest in mining. The claims gave him the right to develop the land, which was much more valuable as commercial real estate.

For his claims to be legal, however, he needed to actually mine the land. Cameron paid little attention to this technicality. He simply "salted" the claims with imported minerals and set up mining equipment to make it look like he was mining. Once his claims were established, Cameron took great pleasure in lording them over the Santa Fe Railroad, who felt *they* had the right to develop the land.

One of Cameron's most contentious claims was located next to the train depot, a spot where he knew the railroad wanted to build a hotel. Cameron built his own hotel there instead. In retaliation, the railroad moved their terminal several hundred feet to the east so train passengers would have to pass the railroad-owned Bright Angel Hotel on their way to Cameron's hotel. Visitation at Cameron's hotel plummeted.

But Cameron had one more trick up his sleeve. His claims also gave him sole control of the Bright Angel Trail, the only trail into the canyon anywhere near Grand Canyon Village. Cameron used this fact to charge $1 a head for every tourist who wanted to descend the trail on horseback. The railroad filed a lawsuit, but Cameron prevailed in court. This time, the railroad went on the offensive, spending thousands of dollars improving the Hermit Trail, located several miles west of the Bright Angel Trail. But Cameron owned mining claims there too, and he howled at the injustice. Tired of his antics, the railroad paid Cameron $40,000 for his bogus mining claims, mostly just to shut him up.

As the years wore on, Cameron lost the will to compete with the railroad, and in 1910 his hotel shut down. But he continued to charge a toll on the Bright Angel Trail. By the time the Park Service finally gained control of the trail, Cameron had leveraged his wealth and power into a seat in the U.S. Senate. For years he continued to fight the park over the legitimacy of his claims. Then, in 1920, the Arizona Supreme Court invalidated his mining claims, a ruling that ultimately ended his real estate empire.

John Hance & Teddy Roosevelt

Park Entrance, 1931

GRAND CANYON NATIONAL PARK

I N FACT, THE wheels had been in motion to create Grand Canyon National Park for quite some time. As early as 1886 Indiana Senator Benjamin Harrison had introduced legislation to preserve Grand Canyon as a national park. At that time there was only one other national park—Yellowstone, created in 1872—and Harrison's legislation sputtered out due to lack of enthusiasm. Two decades later, when Harrison was President, he used his power to establish "Great Canyon Reserve." It was a victory for the Grand Canyon, but many Arizona miners and cattlemen resented the new restrictions placed on the land. They would ultimately provide some of the most vocal opposition to the creation of a national park.

Despite some local opposition, there were many others who saw the need to protect the Grand Canyon. In 1906 the Act for the Preservation of American Antiquities was passed, giving the President the power to set aside areas that held "objects of historic or scientific nature." That same year President Theodore Roosevelt created Grand Canyon Game Reserve. For Roosevelt it was an easy decision. He had visited the Grand Canyon a few years earlier and proclaimed it to be "the most impressive scenery I have ever looked at."

The creation of Grand Canyon Game Reserve was just the beginning. In 1908, Roosevelt established Grand Canyon National Monument, the highest designation a piece of American land can receive without Congressional approval. At that point

Arizona was not yet a state, and it had no Senators or Congressmen to champion the creation of a national park. Then, in 1912, Arizona was admitted to the Union. In 1917 Representative Carl Hayden and Senator Henry Fountain of Arizona introduced legislation to create Grand Canyon National Park. On February 26, 1919 President Woodrow Wilson signed the bill into law.

But creating a national park and running it smoothly were two different matters. Early administration officials lacked a coherent vision for the park, and many major infrastructure issues went unresolved. In its first decade of operation Grand Canyon National Park went through six superintendents. The park needed a strong leader with a long-term commitment to the Grand Canyon. It found that leader in Miner Tillotson, a civil engineer who became superintendent in 1927 and occupied the position for over a decade. Through his tireless efforts he helped shape a coherent administrative vision of the park that set the precedent for years to come.

The same year that Tillotson became superintendent, Congress revised the park's boundaries to include a large portion of Kaibab National Forest. Five years later President Herbert Hoover proclaimed a new Grand Canyon National Monument (the old one had become Grand Canyon National Park) that encompassed 300 square miles in the western Grand Canyon and an additional 40 miles along the Colorado River.

The park was a success on paper, but the flood of new visitors soon overwhelmed the staff. In its first year as a National Park, Grand Canyon received 44,000 visitors. Within a decade, that number had increased to nearly 200,000. In 1937, 300,000 arrived. The numbers kept climbing, but the park's staff remained the same—10 rangers and one park superintendent. It is a testament to the dedication of these early National Park Service employees that such a small staff was able to accommodate so many people. Ultimately, the number of rangers was increased, making the park much more enjoyable for visitors and employees alike.

THE GREAT DAM WARS

B Y THE 1960s the Grand Canyon seemed to be doing just fine. It had a dedicated staff, and millions of people were arriving from all over the world. Movie stars, British royalty, and Arab sheiks all stopped by for a look. The giant hole in the ground that had been avoided for centuries was now one of the nation's most cherished natural landmarks. Best of all, its national park status protected the land from private development. But a massive government project soon threatened to dramatically alter the landscape.

In the early 1960s the U.S. Bureau of Reclamation (the government agency responsible for much of the West's water supply) went looking for a new place to build a dam. Ever since its overwhelming success with Hoover Dam, the Bureau had been building dams at a frantic rate. The West was growing fast, and it needed water to grow, so in the 1930s, '40s, and '50s the Bureau of Reclamation built dams wherever it could. It created huge reservoirs—some the size of small eastern states—that trapped water flowing out to sea. Before long, many of the Southwest's most impressive rivers resembled a string of interconnected reservoirs. By the early 1960s there was only one good place left to build a giant dam: the Grand Canyon.

With its steep walls, deep side canyons, and powerful river, the Grand Canyon was the perfect site for a dam. But there was a catch. Any reservoir created by a dam would be totally impractical from a water-use standpoint. The water would have to be pumped out thousands of feet to bring it to civilization, and the costs involved would be prohibitively expensive. But the Bureau of Reclamation wasn't interested in water.

BY THE 1960S THERE WAS ONLY ONE GOOD PLACE LEFT IN AMERICA TO BUILD A GIANT DAM: THE GRAND CANYON.

It was interested in hydroelectricity. In effect, a dam in the Grand Canyon would be nothing more than a giant cash register to fund other, less economically feasible water projects elsewhere. And the Bureau of Reclamation didn't just want one dam in the Grand Canyon. It wanted two.

When conservationists heard the news they went wild. Conservationists hate dams, a fact that became glaringly apparent in 1948 when the Bureau of Reclamation tried to build a dam along the Green River in Echo Park, Utah. The dam would have flooded part of Dinosaur National Monument, and conservationists were loath to let that happen. Led by David Brower of the Sierra Club, they fought tooth and nail to defeat the dam. They succeeded. But their success came at a huge cost.

As part of the compromise to save Dinosaur National Monument, the two sides agreed upon a new dam farther downstream. The site of the new dam would be Glen Canyon. Lying just north of the Grand Canyon, Glen Canyon was one of the most remote places in the country. Only a few thousand people had ever set eyes on it. So shortly before Glen Canyon Dam was finished, David Brower, the man who had been instrumental in its creation, took a river trip through Glen Canyon to see it for himself. He started to cry.

With its gorgeous sandstone arches, fern covered alcoves, and sweeping river

FLOYD DOMINY

"I like Dave Brower, but I don't think he's the sanctified conservationist that so many people think he is. I think he's a selfish preservationist, for the few. Dave Brower hates my guts. Why? Because I've got guts. I've tangled with Dave Brower for many years."

views, Glen Canyon was one of the most beautiful places Brower had ever seen. In a few months it would all be underwater. Brower would later admit that the creation of Glen Canyon Dam was the greatest failure of his life. From that moment on, he vowed never again to lose another beautiful place to a dam. When he found out that the Bureau of Reclamation wanted to build two more dams in the Grand Canyon, he went into overdrive.

Brower was up against stiff competition. The biggest proponent of the new dams was the head of the Bureau of Reclamation, a man named Floyd Dominy. Dominy had spent his early years helping struggling Wyoming ranchers build dams to save their families from poverty. He knew firsthand how a lack of water could lead to suffering, and he made it his life's mission to build dams. Dominy's drive and ambition were unprecedented. By the time he became head of the Bureau of Reclamation he had many powerful allies, including Arizona Senator Carl Hayden, the chairman of the Appropriations Committee.

Brower versus Dominy. Conservation versus economic growth. The battle over the dams in Grand Canyon soon became much more than a battle for the Grand Canyon. It became a battle for the future of environmental policy in America. For decades economic development had taken precedent over wilderness. But wilderness was disappearing fast, and many people wanted to preserve what was left before it was too late.

Debate over the dams soon shifted into the public arena. Defending the proposed dams, the Bureau of Reclamation argued that the reservoirs would help tourists enjoy the Grand Canyon more fully by allowing tourists to explore previously inaccessible reaches of the Grand Canyon from motorboats. In response, the Sierra Club took out full-page ads in the *New York Times*, the *Los Angeles Times*, the *San Francisco Chronicle*, and the *Washington Post*. The ads read, "Should we also flood the Sistine Chapel so tourists can get nearer the ceiling?"

The response was overwhelming. Letters protesting the dams arrived at the Bureau of Reclamation in dump trucks. Senators and Congressmen were flooded with requests to save the Grand Canyon. The two dams, which would have flooded much of Marble Canyon and the Lower Granite Gorge (including Havasu Creek, the most beautiful place in the canyon), were stopped dead in their tracks.

DAVID BROWER

"Lake Powell is a drag strip for power boats. It's for people who won't do things except the easy way. The magic of Glen Canyon is dead. It has been vulgarized. Putting water in the Cathedral in the Desert was like urinating on the crypt of St. Peter's."

Desert View Watchtower

PARK TODAY

I N 1956 GRAND Canyon's annual visitation passed the 1 million mark. Thirteen years later that number doubled. Twenty years later it tripled. Before long, traffic and pollution had grown to unacceptable levels. In 1974 the Park closed West Rim Drive to private vehicles and began running a free shuttle. The Park also instituted a policy requiring permits and reservations for overnight camping. Before these rules were implemented it was not unusual for upward of 1,000 people to camp near Phantom Ranch, a place that can accommodate about 90 people comfortably.

Today the Grand Canyon receives nearly 5 million visitors annually. To cope with these numbers, the National Park Service has undertaken new measures to alleviate the human pressure on the park. With gridlock, noise, overcrowding, and pollution from auto emissions threatening to interfere with the visitor experience, the Park implemented a General Management Plan that, over time, will keep the Park in as natural a state as possible. Under the plan, private cars will eventually be banned from most areas on the South Rim. Someday visitors will be shuttled around entirely by bus, and possibly by a proposed light rail. Extensive "greenway trails" are being built along the rim for the sole use of bikers and pedestrians. Some commercial and residential activity will be moved away from the rim, and in some cases, out of the Park completely.

But implementation of these changes has been a challenge. With the National Park Service perpetually short of funds, Grand Canyon has had problems coming up with the money. The light rail system alone will cost as much as the entire construction budget of all the national parks combined. But as long as every visitor today makes a conscious effort to appreciate and preserve the Grand Canyon, it will remain a sublime destination for many years to come.

THE
SOUTH RIM

THE SOUTH RIM

THE SOUTH RIM is what most people think of when they think of the Grand Canyon. Here you'll find the park's most famous sights and attractions, as well as most of its lodges, campgrounds, and restaurants. Because the South Rim lies only 60 miles north of Interstate 40 (which runs through Williams and Flagstaff), it's the most accessible—and therefore the most crowded—part of the park. During the peak summer months, congestion can be a bit overwhelming at popular viewpoints, but the crowds die down significantly the rest of the year. (Unlike the North Rim, the South Rim stays open year round.) To help reduce automobile congestion, the park offers a free shuttle service connecting the lodges, park buildings, and popular viewpoints on the South Rim.

The South Rim is divided into three main areas: Grand Canyon Village, Hermit Road, and Desert View Drive. Grand Canyon Village (p.128) is the hub of all tourist activity on the South Rim. Its five lodges—the only ones on the South Rim—accommodate about 1,000 guests, and nearby services including everything from fine dining to auto repair.

Hermit Road (p.150) is a scenic eight-mile stretch of road just west of Grand Canyon Village. It offers some of the finest viewpoints in the park, but it's closed to private vehicle traffic from March 1 to November 30. During those months visitors must use the park's free shuttle service or walk along the Rim Trail, an easy path connecting many of the most popular viewpoints on the South Rim.

Desert View Drive (p.164) heads 25 miles east of Grand Canyon Village to Desert View, a remote yet beautiful outpost in the eastern Grand Canyon. Although there are a number of outstanding viewpoints along Desert View Drive, they tend to be spaced many miles apart with long stretches of forest in between. Desert View Drive is definitely recommended, but it's worth checking out Grand Canyon Village and Hermit Road first.

SOUTH RIM SIGHTS: p.130-179   SOUTH RIM HIKES: p.180-207

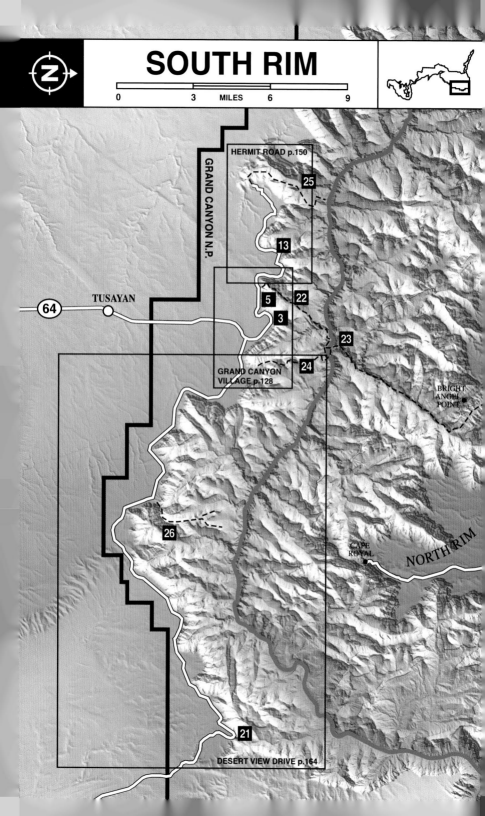

SOUTH RIM

0　　　3　　MILES　　6　　　9

HERMIT ROAD p.150

25

13

GRAND CANYON N.P.

64　TUSAYAN

5

22

3

23

24

BRIGHT ANGEL POINT

GRAND CANYON VILLAGE p.128

26

CAPE ROYAL

NORTH RIM

21

DESERT VIEW DRIVE p.164

SOUTH RIM
HIGHLIGHTS

El Tovar, p.138
The finest hotel in the park, and the best dining.

Bright Angel Trail, p.180
The most popular route to the bottom of the canyon.

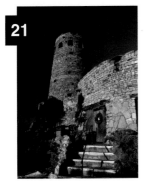

Desert View, p.178
Provides some of the best views in the park.

Yavapai Point, p.135
Panoramic views of the canyon from inside a historic building.

Mohave Point, p.158
Great views of the Colorado River.

SOUTH RIM
HIKING

- **Bright Angel Trail, p.180 (Strenuous, 15.6 miles)**
- **Grandview Trail, p.202 (Strenuous, 6.4 miles)**
- **Hermit Trail, p.196 (Strenuous, 18 miles)**
- **South Kaibab Trail, p.190 (Strenuous, 13.8 miles)**

SOUTH RIM
BASICS

IN THE PARK

INFORMATION

The best place to find seasonal information—shuttle times, ranger programs, etc.—is in the park's free newspaper, *The Guide*. Copies of *The Guide* are available at park entrance stations, visitor centers, and at all lodges. For a more hands-on experience, the Canyon View Information Plaza (p.132) has open-air displays and a ranger-staffed visitor center. Information desks are also found at Yavapai Observation Station (p.135), Kolb Studio (p.148), Tusayan Museum (p.175), and Desert View (p.178).

GETTING TO THE SOUTH RIM

BY CAR

There are two ways to get to the South Rim by car. The first and most popular is the South Entrance Station located about a mile north of the small town of Tusayan (p.125) on State Highway 64. This is the most direct route from Flagstaff and Williams. The second route enters the park via the East Entrance Station on Highway 64 near Desert View. Desert View is located in the remote eastern section of the park, about 25 miles east of Grand Canyon Village.

BY BUS

Open Road Tours and Transportation runs a daily shuttle service from the Amtrak station in Flagstaff to Tusayan and Grand Canyon Village. The cost is $20 one-way for adults, $15 one-way for children.

Telephone: 928-226-8060, 800-766-7117
www.openroadtours.com

BY TRAIN

Grand Canyon Railway runs a daily train from Williams to Grand Canyon Village. Riders travel in vintage railroad cars, some of which are more luxurious (and more expensive) than others. The ride lasts about two hours and features entertainment such as mock hold-ups and singing conductors. The train runs every day of the year except Christmas Eve day and Christmas day.

Telephone: 928-773-1976, 800-843-8724
www.thetrain.com

BY PLANE

Flights from Las Vegas arrive daily at the airport in Tusayan. The two most popular airlines are Scenic Airlines and Air Vegas.

Scenic Airlines
Telephone: 702-638-3300, 800-634-6801
www.scenic.com

Air Vegas
Telephone: 928-638-9351, 800-255-7474
www.airvegas.com

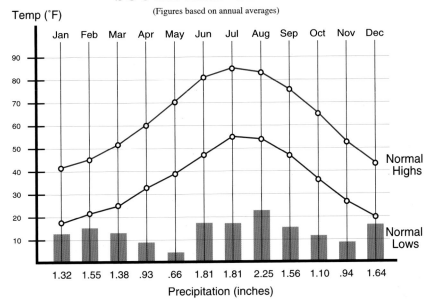

SOUTH RIM CLIMATE
(Figures based on annual averages)

WHEN TO GO

Unlike the North Rim, the South Rim stays open year round. Summer is the most popular time to visit, but the massive crowds combined with the sometimes hot/sometimes rainy weather can diminish your experience. Scorching inner canyon temperatures also make many of the park's most popular trails unbearable in the summer. Despite these hassles, the Grand Canyon remains spectacular. If you have the chance, check out the park in the spring or fall. Both seasons offer cooler temperatures, less rain, and reduced crowds. Spring is also wildflower season, when explosions of color often appear below the rim. Winter brings freezing temperatures and the occasional snowfall. The reduced crowds also create an amazing sense of tranquility (not to mention reduced rates at the park lodges). If you're lucky enough to visit during a snowfall, you'll see the Grand Canyon at its most beautiful.

FEES

The entrance fee for the South Rim (which also gives you access to the North Rim) is $20 per vehicle or $10 per pedestrian, motorcycle rider, or cyclist. Admission is good for seven days. Another option is to purchase a National Parks Pass (also available at the entrance station) for $50 that gives you unlimited access to all U.S. national parks and national monuments for one full year.

WEATHER

South Rim weather varies dramatically from season to season. Summer is hot with daytime highs often topping 80°F. In July, August and early September (monsoon season) short afternoon thundershowers sweep through the Grand Canyon on a regular basis. Winter offers the occasional snowfall, but whatever snow falls usually melts within a few days. Spring and fall are characterized by less precipitation and milder temperatures than summer or winter.

WHAT TO BRING

Clothes: Even summer nights can get chilly on the South Rim, so it's a good idea to pack warm clothes. Rain gear is essential during monsoon season in the late summer. Supplies: Bring supplies for whatever activities interest you (hiking, camping, etc.). Don't worry if you forget to pack basic supplies—there's a large general store in Grand Canyon Village that carries a wide range of groceries, camping supplies, and other gear.

LODGING

All lodging in Grand Canyon National Park is run by Xanterra Parks and Resorts. Reservations should be booked at least several weeks in advance. The most popular rooms on the South Rim—those with canyon views—are sometimes booked as much as two years in advance. All rates listed are based on the peak summer season. Winter rates are often lower by $20–$40.

Reservations: 888-297-2757, outside U.S.: 303-297-2757
www.grandcanyonlodges.com

PHANTOM RANCH

Located at the bottom of the canyon. See page 188.

BRIGHT ANGEL LODGE

This classic lodge is located right on the rim of the canyon. It consists of a main building with several cabins nearby. The lodge offers two types of accommodations: lodge rooms (no TV, some without private bath) and cabin rooms (all with TV and private bath). All rooms have telephones. The lodge's best room is the Bucky O'Neill Suite ($230+ per night), which has a working fireplace and two front doors that open onto the rim. See page 141 for more on Bright Angel Lodge.

Rates: Lodge & cabin rooms: $50+; Cabins on rim: $100–110

EL TOVAR HOTEL

El Tovar offers the finest accommodations in the park. For rustic elegance and historic charm, El Tovar can't be beat. Like the Bright Angel Lodge, El Tovar is located right on the rim of the canyon. Of El Tovar's 75 rooms, three have sweeping canyon views, and several more have partial views of the canyon. All rooms have full bathrooms, air conditioning, cable TV, and telephones. Room service is available during limited hours. See page 138 for more on the El Tovar Hotel.

Rates: Standard: $120-130; Deluxe ; Suites:

KACHINA & THUNDERBIRD LODGES

Kachina Lodge and Thunderbird Lodge are identical modern buildings located between El Tovar Hotel and Bright Angel Lodge. Both buildings are set back about 60 feet from the rim. They offer standard motel-style rooms with two queen beds, TV, telephone, and full bath. Some rooms face the canyon (though there are few actual views) and the rest face the street on the other side of the buildings. Note: Check in at Kachina Lodge is handled by the front desk at the El Tovar Hotel. Check in at Thunderbird Lodge is handled by the front desk at Bright Angel Lodge.

Rates: Canyonside rooms: $120–$130; Streetside rooms: $110–$120

MASWIK LODGE

Maswik Lodge is located 1/4 mile south of the rim of the canyon. It offers motel-style rooms with two queen beds, a full bath, TV, and telephones. The lodge also features a sports bar. Maswik Lodge is divided into a north and south section—rooms in the north section are nicer and more expensive. In the summer, Maswik Lodge also offers rustic cabins with two double beds, shower, TV, and telephone.

Rates: Rustic cabins: $60–$70; South section: $70–$80; North section: $110–$120

YAVAPAI LODGE

Yavapai Lodge is the largest lodge in the park. It's located 1/2 mile away from the rim, making it less popular than other lodges, but the most likely to have rooms available on short notice. All rooms have a full bath, TV, and telephones. Most rooms have two queen beds (some have one king bed). The lodge is divided into Yavapai East and Yavapai West. Rooms in Yavapai East have air conditioning.

Rates: Yavapai East: $100–$110; Yavapai West: $90–$100

CAMPING

MATHER CAMPGROUND

Mather Campground offers year-round tent and RV camping (no hookups). Sites can accommodate up to 2 cars and 6 people. Cost is $15 per night. Reservations can be made up to 5 months in advance and are strongly recommended for Apr.–Nov. The campground is first-come, first-served from Dec–Mar. Group sites accommodating up to 3 cars and 50 people are also available for $40 per night.

Reservations: 800-365-2267; outside U.S.: 301-722-1257
www.reservations.nps.gov

DESERT VIEW CAMPGROUND

Desert View Campground is located at Desert View (p.178), 25 miles east of Grand Canyon Village at the end of Desert View Drive. The campground is open from mid-May through mid-October. Sites are available on a first-come, first-served basis. Each site accommodates up to 2 cars and 6 people. Cost is $10 per night.

TRAILER VILLAGE

Trailer Village is an RV campground with hookups located next to Mather Campground. It accommodates RVs up to 50 feet in length. Cost is $24 per night for 2 people ($2 for each additional adult). Open year round. Reservations are handled by Xanterra and are highly recommended for April–October.

Reservations: Advance: 888-297-2757, Same-day: 928-638-2631
www.grandcanyonlodges.com

GETTING AROUND

BY CAR

Many people choose to explore the South Rim by car, but traffic and a lack of parking at major attractions can sometimes be unbearable during the busy summer months. There are five major parking areas in Grand Canyon Village, all of which are mapped out in *The Guide*. The largest is lot B (located in Market Plaza), and the closest to the rim is lot D (across from the train depot). Note: From March 1 through November 30, Hermit Road and the road to Yaki Point/South Kaibab Trailhead are closed to private vehicle traffic. During this time, Hermit Drive and Yaki Point/South Kaibab Trailhead are accessible via the park's free shuttles.

BY SHUTTLE

The park offers a free shuttle system that stops at most of the South Rim's most popular sites. Up to date seasonal shuttle schedules are listed in *The Guide*.

Village Shuttle
This route provides transportation between Canyon View Information Plaza, Yavapai Point, Mather Campground, and all hotels and parking lots in Grand Canyon Village.

Hermit Rest Route
This route, along Hermit Drive, operates from March 1 through November 30 with stops at eight major canyon overlooks. Departs from the Hermits Rest Interchange near Bright Angel Lodge.

Kaibab Trail Route
This route runs between the Canyon View Information Plaza and Yaki Point/ South Kaibab Trailhead.

Hiker's Express Route
This early morning shuttle departs from Bright Angel Lodge and the Backcountry Information Center and heads directly to the South Kaibab Trailhead.

ON FOOT

The area around Grand Canyon Village is the only place that's practical to explore on foot without going on an extended hike along the rim. If an extended hike along the rim is what you're looking for, however, head for the Rim Trail. More of a walk than a hike, the Rim Trail runs from Pipe Creek Vista (about a half mile south of Yaki Point, p.166) to Hermits Rest (p.162) and stops at every major viewpoint along the way. All told, the Rim Trail is about 13 miles long. It's paved for the 3.5 miles between Pipe Creek Vista and Maricopa Point (p.152).

BY BICYCLE

Bicycles are allowed on all paved and unpaved roads on the South Rim, but they are prohibited from all other trails, including the Rim Trail. If you don't mind the traffic on major roads, bicycles are one of the best ways to explore the overlooks along the South Rim. Bicyclists must obey all traffic regulations. While riding on the narrow Hermit Road, bicyclists should pull to the right shoulder of the road and dismount when large vehicles are attempting to pass.

BY TAXI

A 24-hour taxi service is available on the South Rim. Telephone: 928-638-2822

DINING

With the exception of a cafeteria at Desert View and a snack shop at Hermits Rest, all dining establishments on the South Rim are located in Grand Canyon Village. During the busy summer months, restaurants that don't accept reservations can fill up fast and wait times can exceed two hours. To beat the crowds, try to arrive before sunset.

ARIZONA ROOM

Standard/upscale American fare. Located in Bright Angel Lodge. Only serves dinner from 4:30–10pm. No reservations accepted. Telephone: 928-638-2526 Ext. 6296

BRIGHT ANGEL RESTAURANT

Standard American fare. Located in Bright Angel Lodge. Serves breakfast, lunch, and dinner from 6:30am–10pm. No reservations accepted. Telephone: 928-638-2526 Ext. 6189

EL TOVAR

The finest and most expensive dining in the park—prices often top $20 an entree. Soft lighting and dark wood paneling round out the elegant atmosphere. Reservations are only available for dinner and are usually made days in advance. Open for breakfast (6:30am–11am), lunch (11:30am–2pm), and dinner (5–10pm). Telephone: 928-638-2526 Ext. 6432

MASWIK CAFETERIA

Cafeteria-style fast food with Mexican and Italian selections. Open 6am-10pm.

YAVAPAI CAFETERIA

Cafeteria-style fast food. Open 6am–9pm in summer; 7am–8pm the rest of the year.

ENTERTAINMENT

RANGER PROGRAMS

The National Park Service offers free ranger programs that are highly recommended. Topics cover a wide range of subjects including history, geology, wildlife, and more. Check *The Guide* for times and listings.

BUS TOURS

Xanterra offers narrated bus tours along the South Rim. The Desert View Tour along Desert View Drive lasts about four hours and costs $27.50. The Hermit Road Tour along Hermits Drive lasts about two hours and costs $15.50. Sunrise and sunset tours ($12) are also available from May through October. Children under 16 ride for free on all bus tours. A package deal offering two tours for $32.50 is also available. For additional information contact the transportation desk at any lodge.

Telephone: 928-638-2631
www.grandcanyonlodges.com

MULE TRIPS

Day and overnight mule trips depart daily from the South Rim. Day trips descend 3,500 feet down the Bright Angel Trail (p.180) to Plateau Point (p.186) and return via the same route. The trip takes about seven hours and costs $130 per person. Overnight trips follow Bright Angel Trail to the bottom of the canyon where riders spend the night at Phantom Ranch (p.188), then return the next day via the South Kaibab Trail (p.190). Cost is $350 for one person, $625 for two people. Rides offering an extra night at Phantom Ranch are available from November through March. Cost is $495 for one person, $835 for two people. Reservations for mule trips during the summer and holidays should be made as far in advance as possible—they are accepted up to one year in advance. Due to cancellations last minute reservations are sometimes available, if you put your name on a waiting list 24 hours beforehand and show up at 6am on the day of the trip.

Telephone: 928-638-2631
www.grandcanyonlodges.com

ART EXHIBITS

Kolb Studio (p.148) features a constantly changing art exhibit. Check *The Guide* for a listing of the exhibit currently on display.

GRAND CANYON MUSIC FESTIVAL

This annual chamber music festival is held in September at the Shrine of the Ages. Inquire at any information center for additional details.
www.grandcanyonmusic

SERVICES

CANYON VILLAGE MARKETPLACE

This general store in Market Plaza sells groceries, sandwiches, film, and a wide variety of other items. Camping equipment and outdoor gear is also sold and rented. Open 7am–8:30pm in the summer, 8am–7pm the rest of the year.

GAS

There are no gas stations in Grand Canyon Village. The closest gas stations are located in Tusayan and at Desert View.

BANK

Located in Market Plaza. A 24-hour ATM is available. The bank does not exchange foreign currency or cash out-of-town checks. Open Monday–Friday. Telephone: 928-638-2437

POST OFFICE

Located in Market Plaza. Open Monday–Friday 9am–5pm. Open Sat. 11am–3pm. Telephone: 928-638-2512

COIN-OPERATED SHOWERS & LAUNDROMAT

Located near the entrance to Mather Campground. Open summer 6am–11pm; spring and fall 7am–9pm; winter 8am-6pm.

PET KENNEL

Provides lodging for pets that aren't allowed in park lodges or on inner canyon trails. Open daily 7:30am–5pm. Reservations are recommended. The kennel also has homeless animals for adoption. Telephone: 928-638-0534

GRAND CANYON GARAGE

Located in Grand Canyon Village. Offers auto repair from 8am–noon and 1–5pm daily. Emergency 24-hour service and towing is also available. Telephone: 928-638-2631

LOST AND FOUND

For items lost or found in hotels or restaurants call 928-638-2631
For items lost or found anywhere else call 928-638-7798

OUTSIDE THE PARK

TUSAYAN

Tusayan is a small town located about one mile south of the park entrance station. It consists of a short stretch of hotels, restaurants, and stores lining either side of Highway 64. The town's most notable features are its IMAX movie theater and airport—the second busiest in the state due to the large number of sightseeing flights.

LODGING (Tusayan)

Surprisingly, lodging in Tusayan is often more expensive than lodging in Grand Canyon Village. The reason: Many of Tusayan's hotels offer modern luxuries such as swimming pools and spas that are unavailable in the park. Room rates listed below refer to peak tourist season. Rates usually drop in the winter.

BEST WESTERN GRAND CANYON SQUIRE INN
The most extravagant option in Tusayan. Offers large rooms, outdoor pool, tennis courts, spa, sports bar, three restaurants, and a six-lane bowling alley.
Rates: $135+
Telephone: 928-638-2681, 800-622-6966
www.grandcanyonsquire.com

GRAND CANYON QUALITY INN AND SUITES
Standard chain motel. Offers outdoor pool and a large indoor hot tub.
Rates: $135+
Telephone: 928-638-2673, 800-221-2222
www.grandcanyonqualityinn.com

THE GRAND HOTEL
A modern hotel with a classic lodge design. Offers an indoor pool, a large restaurant, and entertainment featuring Native American dancers and cowboy singers.
Rates: $149+
Telephone: 888-634-7263
www.visitgrandcanyon.com

HOLIDAY INN EXPRESS
Standard chain motel. Offers an indoor pool, spa, free continental breakfast, and Kids Suites with bunk beds, TV, VCR, and video games.
Rates: 139+
Telephone: 928-638-3000, 888-473-2269
www.gcanyon.com/hi

LODGING (Tusayan)

RODEWAY INN RED FEATHER LODGE
Budget motel. Offers outdoor pool, hot tub, and fitness center.
Rates: $79+
Telephone: 928-638-2414, 800-538-2345
www.redfeatherlodge.com

SEVEN MILE LODGE
Budget motel. Only offers 20 rooms, but it's the cheapest option in Tusayan.
Rates: $68+
Telephone: 928-638-2291

CAMPING (Tusayan)

GRAND CANYON CAMPER VILLAGE
Grand Canyon Camper Village offers tent and RV sites. Tent sites cost $18 per night. RV sites cost $22+ per night. Coin-operated showers and a playground for kids are also offered. Reservations are only available for RV sites with hookups.
Telephone: 928-638-2887

TEN X CAMPGROUND
Open May through September. Cost is $10 per vehicle. Located two miles south of Tusayan. Operated by the Kaibab National Forest.
Telephone: 928-638-2443

DINING (Tusayan)

CAFE TUSAYAN
Classic American fare. Located next to the Red Feather Lodge. Open for breakfast, lunch, and dinner.
Telephone: 928-638-2150

CANYON STAR
Classic American fare and Southwestern dishes. Located in The Grand Hotel. Open for breakfast, lunch, and dinner (buffet options in the summer).
Telephone: 928-638-3333

CORONADO ROOM
Classic American fare and Southwestern dishes. Located in the Best Western Grand Canyon Squire. Open only for dinner.
Telephone: 928-638-2681

FAST FOOD
McDonald's, Wendy's, Taco Bell, and Pizza Hut are all present in Tusayan.

THE YIPPEI-EI-O! STEAKHOUSE
Classic steakhouse. Open for lunch (summer only) and dinner.
Telephone: 928-638-2780

WE COOK PIZZA AND PASTA
Serves, you guessed it, pizza and pasta. Open for lunch and dinner.
Telephone: 928-638-2278

ENTERTAINMENT (Tusayan)

IMAX THEATER
Year after year, the IMAX movie *Grand Canyon—The Hidden Secrets* lures hordes of visitors into this air-conditioned theater. The narrative can be a bit tacky, but the scenery is undeniably breathtaking—made all the more so by the massive 70-foot screen. The 35-minute movie plays every hour on the half hour. Open 8:30am–9:30pm March-October, 10:30am–6:30pm November-February.
Cost: $10 adults, $7 children under 12.

SCENIC FLIGHTS
Scenic flights over the Grand Canyon are incredibly popular—so much so that limits have been placed on the number of flights allowed each year, and flights are prohibited from flying over 75 percent of the park. At issue is the noise created by the flights and its impact on the wilderness experience of hikers and river runners. Controversy aside, scenic flights offer a breathtaking perspective unlike anything found on the rim. Both helicopter and airplane flights are offered. Most people prefer helicopters because they fly near rim level and offer up-close views of the canyon. Airplanes, which fly about 1,000 feet higher due to air-space regulations, generally cost less.

HELICOPTER FLIGHTS

AirStar Helicopters
Telephone: 800-962-3869
www.airstar.com

Papillon
Telephone: 800-528-2418
www.papillon.com

Grand Canyon Helicopters
Telephone: 800-541-4537
www.grandcanyonhelicoptersaz.com

AIRPLANE FLIGHTS

Air Grand Canyon
Telephone: 800-247-4726
www.airgrandcanyon.com

Grand Canyon Airlines
Telephone: 866-235-9422
www.grandcanyonairlines.com

GRAND CANYON VILLAGE

THE BATTLESHIP

INDIAN GARDEN
CAMPGROUND

POWELL
POINT

11
10 MARICOPA
POINT

22 BRIGHT
ANGEL
TRAIL

YAVAPAI
POINT

3
P

HERMIT ROAD

RIM TRAIL

EL TOVAR
HOPI HOUSE

9 **8**
P **6** **5** **4**

P **7**

P

PARK HQ

SHRINE OF
THE AGES

P YAVAPAI
LODGE

MASWIK
LODGE

BACKCOUNTRY
OFFICE

MARKET
PLAZA

CENTER ROAD

CLINIC
✚

MATHER
CAMPGROUND

P Publlic Parking

TONTO TRAIL

SOUTH
KAIBAB
TRAIL 24

MATHER
POINT 1

2

CANYON VIEW
INFORMATION
PLAZA

YAKI
POINT

16

TRAILER
VILLAGE

DESERT VIEW DRIVE

O'Neill Butte

1 MATHER POINT

Mather Point is the most popular viewpoint in the park, but that's only because of its location. This is the closest viewpoint to the park entrance. Still, the views are fantastic. Amazingly, only about a third of the total length of the Grand Canyon is visible from here—a fact that speaks volumes about the size of the canyon.

Among the famous canyon landmarks visible from Mather Point are O'Neill Butte (above) and Vishnu Temple (left). Vishnu Temple rises to a height of 7,533 feet. It was named by the early geologist Clarence Dutton who felt it had "a surprising resemblance to an Oriental pagoda."

Mather Point is named for Stephen Mather, a retired millionaire who in 1914 complained to Interior Secretary Franklin Lane about the management of America's national parks. Lane responded, "...if you don't like the way the national parks are being run, come on down to Washington and run them yourself." Mather did just that. In 1916, he became the first director of the National Park Service and spent the next 13 years of his life shaping a cohesive vision for America's national parks.

Although the views from Mather Point are stunning, it's one of the most congested spots in the park. This is especially true in the summer. Savvy visitors know that there are equally fantastic viewpoints to the east (Yaki Point, p.166) and west (Yavapai Point, p.135). So if the crowds are overwhelming at Mather Point, it's probably best to skip it for now and come back later on.

NOTE: Parking is limited to 60 minutes at Mather Point.

Vishnu Temple

2 *CANYON VIEW INFO PLAZA*

This complex of buildings is nestled in the woods across the road from Mather Point. (Ironically, there is no view at Canyon View Information Plaza.) Because of its proximity to the park entrance, it serves as the park's main welcoming center.

The visitor center at Canyon View Information Plaza offers a ranger-staffed help desk and many useful exhibits about the park. Across the way is Books & More, a store operated by the non-profit Grand Canyon Association. It offers a wide range of books, maps, postcards, etc. Rest rooms are also located nearby.

Canyon View Information Plaza opened in 2000. It was originally intended to be the terminus of a light rail system that would run from large parking lots in Tusayan. Visitors would leave their cars in Tusayan, hop the train to Canyon View Information Plaza, and then travel around the South Rim via the park's free shuttle system. (The open air exhibits were built to give visitors something to look at while they waited for the train.) For the moment, however, the light rail project has been postponed.

Canyon View Information Plaza is open 8am–6pm from May through mid-October and 8am–5pm the rest of the year.

Telephone: 928-638-7888

NOTE: There's no parking at Canyon View Information Plaza. The closest parking is at Mather Point. You can also park in Grand Canyon Village and hop a free shuttle back to Canyon View Information Plaza or use the new pedestrian and biking trail—the Greenway Trail—between Grand Canyon Village and the plaza.

Bright Angel Canyon

Yavapai Observation Station

3 YAVAPAI POINT

Yavapai Point is home to the Yavapai Observation Station, which served as the South Rim's first museum and interpretive center. The building was originally built in 1928. It has large viewing windows providing sweeping panoramas of the canyon, making it one of the best places to visit in bad weather. The building also houses a small store that sells books, posters, and postcards.

One of the most prominent features visible from Yavapai Point is Bright Angel Canyon, which cuts back eight miles into the North Rim. The North Kaibab Trail (p.296) runs along much of Bright Angel Canyon. As the trail approaches the Colorado River, it passes by Phantom Ranch, a collection of small buildings offering the only overnight lodging at the bottom of the canyon. Phantom Ranch is faintly visible from Yavapai Point—look for the green patch of foliage near the end of Bright Angel Canyon, just north of the Colorado River.

Several famous canyon features are visible from Yavapai Point. Just above the dark Inner Gorge at the bottom of the canyon lies the broad, flat Tonto Platform. Eagle-eyed visitors can spot the faint Tonto Trail running east-west along the Tonto Platform on the south of the river.

Yavapai is a Paiute word that means "sun people." It refers to a group of Indians that historically lived in central and western Arizona.

NOTE: Rest rooms are located in a small building just south of Yavapai Observation Center, next to the parking lot.

4 *HOPI HOUSE*

Hopi House was designed by renowned architect Mary Colter, who designed many of the park's famous historic buildings. This structure was her first building assignment in the park. She patterned it after buildings at Old Orabai, a Hopi village 80 miles east of Grand Canyon that is the oldest continuously inhabited town in America. The stone exterior, corner fireplaces, and thatched ceilings are all characteristic of Hopi structures. The building officially opened in 1905. Hopi Indians helped in its construction and traditional Hopi craftsmen lived on its upper floors for many years. Nightly Hopi dances (right) were also common during this time. Today crafts from several tribes are sold inside.

MARY COLTER

AT A TIME when few women practiced archictecture, Mary Colter designed some of the most famous buildings in the Southwest. She worked for the Fred Harvey Company between 1902 and 1948, and many of her buildings are now listed as historic landmarks. Among her Grand Canyon creations: Lookout Studio (p.146), Hermit's Rest (p.162), Desert View Watchtower (p.178), and Phantom Ranch (p.188).

5 EL TOVAR HOTEL

El Tovar is the finest hotel in the Grand Canyon. Designed by architect Charles Whittlesey, it was one of the most luxurious hotels in the Southwest when it first opened in 1905. Its modern amenities included steam heat, indoor plumbing, cold *and* hot water, and electric lights—a stark contrast to the primitive rooms, cheap beds, and outhouses that had previously defined luxury at the Grand Canyon. When it first opened, El Tovar's 100 rooms doubled the total number of hotel rooms on the South Rim. For many years fresh fruits and vegetables were grown in El Tovar's greenhouses, and hotel farm animals provided fresh milk and eggs.

El Tovar was named after Don Pedro de Tovar, a lieutenant of Spanish explorer Francisco Vasquez de Coronado who led the first Spanish expedition through the Southwest in 1540 (p.81). Ironically, Don Pedro de Tovar never set eyes on the Grand Canyon. That feat was accomplished by another of Cortes' men, Garcia Lopez de Cardenas. But the Fred Harvey Company—the owner of the El Tovar Hotel—already had a Cardenas Hotel in Trinidad, Colorado. To avoid confusion, the name El Tovar was chosen for the new hotel.

Since its construction, El Tovar has played host to such 20th century icons as Theodore Roosevelt, Albert Einstein, and Paul McCartney. Today the hotel continues to offer the finest lodging and dining in the park. Even if you're not a guest, El Tovar is worth a quick look inside the front lobby or a long drink at the hotel bar.

6   BRIGHT ANGEL LODGE

Back when Bright Angel Lodge first opened in 1896, it consisted of nothing more than a collection of primitive tents. Visitors walked from tent to tent along an elevated boardwalk that protected them from horse and mule droppings—a prominent feature in Grand Canyon Village back then. Over the years the lodge expanded to include a log and frame building with eight guest rooms. Tents were rented for $1.50 per night, and hotel rooms were rented for $2.50 per night. The current lodge dates from the 1930s.

Bright Angel Lodge continues to offer some of the best budget lodging in Grand Canyon Village. It's also the closest lodge to the Bright Angel Trail, which is located about 50 yards to the west (something worth considering if you're looking for a place to stay after a grueling hike on the Bright Angel Trail). The lodge also offers a gift shop, restaurant, bar, and small museum open to the public. A small booth to the left of the front desk also offers information on ranger tours, bus tours, mule rides, and other daily activities.

NOTE: The small museum in Bright Angel Lodge contains a fireplace built out of Grand Canyon rocks—arranged floor to ceiling in their proper geologic sequence.

View near Bright Angel Lodge

7 SANTA FE TRAIN DEPOT

The Santa Fe Railroad Depot is located just south of the El Tovar Hotel. It's the only rail station in any U.S. national park and the last surviving train depot in the United States built out of logs.

The first train arrived at the South Rim in 1901, following the completion of a spur line from the town of Williams, 60 miles to the south. Before then the most dependable form of transportation to the rim was a bumpy, all-day stagecoach ride that cost $20. When the railroad was finished, visitors could travel to the Grand Canyon in about four hours for $3.50. The railroad brought a flood of new visitors to the South Rim, but within a few decades most people were arriving by car. In 1968 falling ridership forced the railroad to shut down—the last departing train carried only three passengers. But in 1989 the railroad roared back to life. With traffic and congestion increasing in the park, a new generation of riders rediscovered the railroad's convenience and charm. Today trains depart daily from Williams (p.117).

The new train

8 LOOKOUT STUDIO

Lookout Studio is a pretty little building perched right at the edge of the canyon, just west of Bright Angel Lodge. The building was designed by Mary Colter, whose goal was to have it blend seamlessly into the landscape, creating as little visual disturbance with the scenery as possible. This followed the design principles set forth by renowned landscape architect Fredrick Law Olmstead. He believed that, whenever possible, buildings in national parks should reflect the architecture of indigenous cultures. The indigenous cultures of the Southwest had built some of the most impressive buildings in ancient America, and Colter incorporated many of their architectural techniques—stone walls, flat roofs, timber supports—into her design.

An old Santa Fe Railroad brochure boasted that visitors who peered through the telescopes at Lookout Studio could, "traverse the Canyon trails, explore the rugged portions of the interior, or see its faraway reaches." Such pastimes continue to lure visitors today. In addition to its stunning views, Lookout Studio offers a small gift shop inside.

Lookout Studio, 1915

9 *KOLB STUDIO*

For over 70 years Kolb Studio was the home of Emery Kolb, who arrived here with his brother Ellsworth in 1902. Shortly after their arrival, the brothers set up a photography studio on the rim and started hawking souvenir photos of mule riders descending the nearby Bright Angel Trail. But as *Saturday Evening Post* writer Irvin S. Cobb wrote of one such mule ride, "Just under the first terrace a halt is made while the official photographer takes a picture; and when you get back he has your finished copy ready for you, so you can see for yourself just how pale and haggard and wall-eyed and how much like a typhoid patient you looked."

Although tourist photos paid the bills, the Kolb's true passion was exploring the Grand Canyon and capturing their daredevil exploits on film (right). In 1911 the brothers ran the Colorado River from Wyoming to California—the first time anyone had accomplished this feat since Powell's historic journey in 1869. But their trip wasn't just for the record books. The Kolbs filmed their voyage and made the first movie of a river trip through the Grand Canyon. It became an instant classic. The Kolbs screened their movie at lectures across the country, and it played continuously at Kolb Studio until Emery's death in 1976.

Today Kolb Studio houses a bookstore and an art gallery with changing exhibits.

Emery Kolb

HERMIT ROAD

TRAVERTINE CANYON

ERMITA MESA

HERMIT GORGE

PIMA
POINT
6799' **14**

25 HERMIT
TRAIL

HERMITS
REST **15**

RIM TRAIL

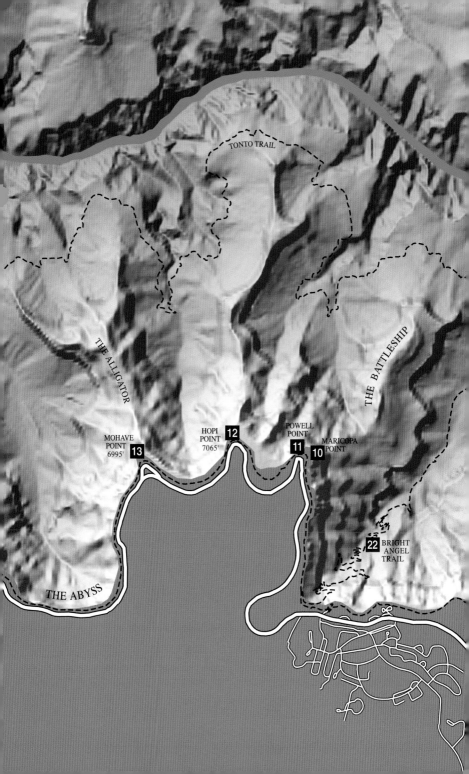

TONTO TRAIL

THE ALLIGATOR

THE BATTLESHIP

MOHAVE
POINT
6995' **13**

HOPI
POINT **12**
7065'

POWELL
POINT **11**
        10 MARICOPA
              POINT

        22 BRIGHT
              ANGEL
              TRAIL

THE ABYSS

10 MARICOPA POINT

Maricopa Point offers the first sweeping views of the western Grand Canyon on Hermit Road. To the west of the point is a large metal frame that marks the remains of the Lost Orphan Mine. In the 1950s, the Lost Orphan Mine was the most productive uranium mine in America. Several decades earlier, a privately owned resort was located on the same spot. It consisted of 20 cabins, a trading post, and a saloon. For a short while the resort was owned by Will Rogers, Jr., who named it "Roger's Place."

"Imagine, if you can, a monster of a hollow approximately some hundreds of miles long and a mile deep, and anywhere from ten to sixteen miles wide, with a mountain range—the most wonderful mountain range in the world—planted in it . . . Imagine all this spread out beneath the unflawed turquoise of the Arizona sky and washed in the liquid gold of the Arizona sunshine—and if you imagine hard enough and keep it up long enough you may begin, in the course of eight or ten years, to have a faint, a very faint and shadowy conception of this spot where the shamed scheme of creation is turned upside down and the very womb of the world is laid bare before our imperious eyes. Then go to Arizona and see it all for yourself, and you will realize what an entirely inadequate and deficient thing the human imagination is."

—Irvin S. Cobb, *Roughing It, Deluxe*, 1913

11 POWELL POINT

Powell Point is named for John Wesley Powell, the famous one-armed explorer who led the first Colorado River expedition through the Grand Canyon in 1869. In 1920 a monument to Powell (left) was dedicated here. The ceremony was attended by Powell's niece and grand-niece, and the monument was christened by the Secretary of the Interior with water from the Colorado River.

Powell's journey through the Grand Canyon is often referred to as the last great expedition of the American West. Before his trip, no one knew what lay at the bottom of the canyon—or along much of the Colorado River for that matter. There were rumors of giant waterfalls and places where the river disappeared underground. Accepting these risks, Powell and nine other men (none with any significant whitewater experience) launched four boats from Green River, Wyoming, in May 1869. Ninety-nine days later, two boats carrying six skeletal men emerged from the Grand Canyon near present-day Lake Mead. Four men had abandoned the grueling journey along the way—three of the four died trying to reach civilization. The names of those four men do not appear on the monument. For more on Powell's extraordinary journey, see page XX.

Shiva Temple   Isis Temple

12 *HOPI POINT*

Hopi Point offers some of the most sweeping views of the canyon on Hermit Road. It was named in honor of the Hopi Indians (p.78).

Several famous geologic features are visible from Hopi Point, including Shiva Temple, named for the Hindu destroyer; Isis Temple, named for the Egyptian goddess of nature; and Cheops Pyramid, named for the Great Pyramid of Cheops. Shiva Temple was named by 19th-century geologist Clarence Dutton who wrote, "In such a stupendous scene of wreck it seems as if the fabled 'Destroyer' might find an abode not wholly uncongenial." Shiva Temple is the largest of the North Rim buttes, rising 4,000 feet from its base with a 300-acre flat top. This so-called "sky island" has probably been separated from the North Rim for over 100,000 years. Today hardcore rock climbers love scaling Shiva Temple's steep walls.

NOTE: Hopi Point is one of the best places to see sunset on Hermit Road.

Cheops Pyramid

 "At length, as the sun draws near the horizon, the great drama of the day begins . . . Slowly the myriad of details have come out and the walls are flecked with lines of minute tracery . . . Stronger and sharper becomes the relief of each projection . . . The colossal buttes expand in every dimension. Their long, narrow wings, which once were folded together and flattened against each other, open out, disclosing between them vast alcoves illuminated with Rembrandt lights . . . A thousand forms, hitherto unseen or obscure, start up within the abyss, and stand forth in strength and animation. All things seem to grow in beauty, power, and dimensions. What was grand before has become majestic, the majestic becomes sublime, and, ever expanding and developing, the sublime passes beyond the reach of our faculties and becomes transcendent."

—Clarence Dutton,
A Tertiary History of the Grand Canyon District, 1882

13 MOHAVE POINT

Mohave Point is named in honor of the Mojave Indians, who once lived along the lower Colorado River south of the Grand Canyon. And no, that's not a typo you just saw. As a general rule, Mojave is spelled with a "j" when referring to place names in California, and with an "h" when referring to place names in Arizona.

The long promontory that stretches down from Mohave Point (right) is called the Alligator. It was named by long-time Canyon resident Emery Kolb, who thought the low ridge looked like the back of an alligator.

Hermit Rapid (above) is visible from Mohave Point. The rapid formed when debris washed into the river from the adjacent side canyon. It's possible to hike to Hermit Rapid from Hermits Rest (p.162) along the Hermit Trail (p.196).

"Imagine, way down there at the bottom, a stream visible only at certain favored points because of the mighty intervening ribs and chines of rock—a stream that appears to you as a torpidly crawling yellow worm, its wrinkling back spangled with tarnished white specks, but which is really a wide, deep, brawling, rushing river—the Colorado—full of torrents and rapids; and those white specks you see are the tops of enormous rocks in its bed."

—Irvin S. Cobb, *Roughing It, Deluxe*, 1913

Hermit Rapids

14 *PIMA POINT*

Pima Point offers one of the best views of the Colorado River along the South Rim. It was named after the Pima Indians of southern Arizona. Although the Pima refer to themselves as *Akimel O'odham*, "River People," the name Pima is derived from *pim'ach*, which means "I don't understand you." This was probably the unfortunate response given to the first Spanish explorers when they asked the *Akimel O'odham* what they called themselves.

In 1912 the Fred Harvey Company built an upscale camp named Hermit Camp (right) 3,600 feet below Pima Point. Hermit Camp was located along the Hermit Trail—the Santa Fe Railroad's free alternative to the Bright Angel Trail, which was then operated as a private toll road (p.100). The camp boasted such amenities as tent cabins, showers, and telephones. A dining hall, stable, and blacksmith's shop were also located on the premises. Guests often stayed for several days, spending their time exploring the rugged area on foot or horseback.

In 1926 an aerial tram was built between Pima Point and Hermit Camp. At the time, it was the longest single-span tram (6,300 feet) in the United States. Travel time was about a half hour each way. But this modern marvel did not last long. In the late 1920s the park service gained control of the Bright Angel Trail and lifted its toll. Soon, most visitors were descending the canyon via the Bright Angel Trail—or the newly completed South Kaibab Trail—and staying at Phantom Ranch. Visitation at Hermit Camp plummeted. In 1930 the camp shut down. A few years later, its remains were burned and the tram was removed.

Hermit Camp

15 *HERMITS REST*

Hermits Rest marks the end of Hermit Road. Its main attraction is a whimsical stone building with a gift shop inside. Drinks, snacks, and rest rooms are also available.

Hermits Rest was built by the Santa Fe Railroad in 1914. Like many famous buildings in the park, it was designed by Mary Colter, whose goal was to create a building that looked as if a hermit might live there. In addition to the main building—famous for its large fireplace—she designed a limestone arch that greets visitors with an authentic New Mexican mission bell.

Hermits Rest was inspired by an early prospector named Louis Boucher, who lived by himself in the canyon below. Although he was labeled a hermit, Boucher was, by all accounts, quite a friendly man. He simply preferred living alone. Originally from Quebec, Boucher arrived at the Grand Canyon around 1891. He lived with a variety of animals including horses, mules, and goldfish, which he kept in a trough. Boucher also planted an orchard that provided him with peaches, oranges, and figs. After spending two decades searching in vain for a rich mineral strike, Boucher moved to Utah in 1909.

Louis Boucher

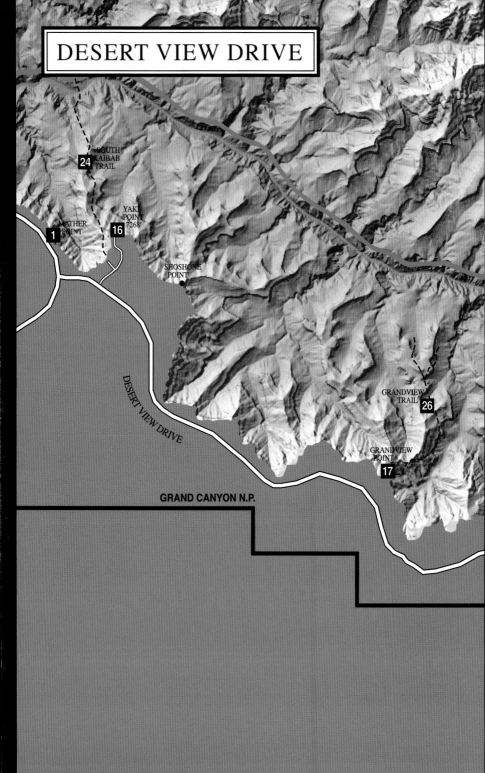

DESERT VIEW DRIVE

SOUTH
KAIBAB
TRAIL

24

MATHER
POINT

1

YAKI
POINT
7268'

16

SHOSHONE
POINT

DESERT VIEW DRIVE

GRANDVIEW
TRAIL

26

GRANDVIEW
POINT

17

GRAND CANYON N.P.

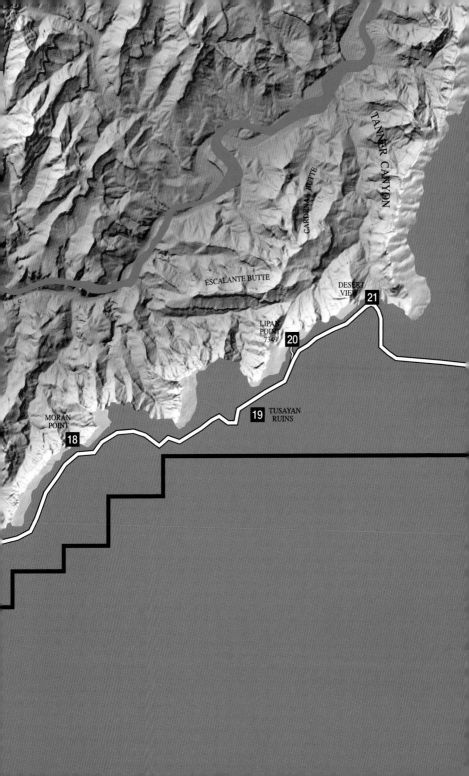

TANNER CANYON

CARDENAS BUTTE

ESCALANTE BUTTE

DESERT
VIEW

LIPAN
POINT
7349

21

20

19   TUSAYAN
RUINS

MORAN
POINT

18

16 *YAKI POINT*

Yaki Point is one of the best places to watch sunrise on the South Rim. It stretches out far into the canyon, providing sweeping views to the east and west. The South Kaibab Trail (p.190) departs just south of Yaki Point. The trail—one of the few in the park that does not follow a historic Indian path—offers the most direct route to the bottom of the canyon from any point on the South Rim.

Yaki Point was supposedly named by George Wharton James in honor of Mexico's Yaqui Indians—the victims of mass genocide in the late 1900s.

NOTE: Unless you are visiting in the winter, the entrance to Yaki Point will be closed to private traffic and can only be reached via the park's free shuttle.

"Imagine—if it be winter—snowdrifts above, with desert flowers blooming alongside the drifts, and down below great stretches of green verdure; imagine two or three separate snowstorms visibly raging at different points, with clear, bright stretches of distance intervening between them, and nearer maybe a splendid rainbow arching downward into the great void; for these meteorological three-ring circuses are not uncommon at certain seasons."

—Irvin S. Cobb, *Roughing It, Deluxe,* 1913

Grandview Hotel

17 GRANDVIEW POINT

Grandview Point is one of the highest points on the South Rim (7,406 feet) which accounts for its name. Its altitude also explains why there are so many ponderosa pines—which thrive at high elevations—growing nearby.

Before the railroad arrived at Grand Canyon Village, Grandview Point was the hub of all tourist activity on the South Rim. In 1886 John Hance—a prospector turned tour guide (p.92)—built the first hotel here. A few years later, another prospector named Pete Berry built the Grandview Hotel nearby (above). But when the railroad arrived at Grand Canyon Village in 1901, few visitors were willing to make the additional trek to Grandview Point. By 1908 all hotel operations at Grandview Point had shut down. A few years later, Berry sold his land holdings to legendary newspaperman William Randolph Hearst. Hearst tore down the Grandview Hotel in 1929 and considered building a new hotel on the property, but a federal court forced him to sell his land to the park in 1939.

During its short-lived hotel era, Grandview Point was also the jumping off point for a number of mines located below the rim. In 1890 Pete Berry, Ralph Cameron (p.100), and Niles Cameron established the Last Chance copper mine at Horseshoe Mesa, just below Grandview Point. The mine contained an extremely high grade ore—up to 70 percent copper—but when the price of copper crashed in 1907, all mining operations at the Last Chance mine were forced to shut down.

NOTE: Grandview Point is the start of the Grandview Trail (p.202).

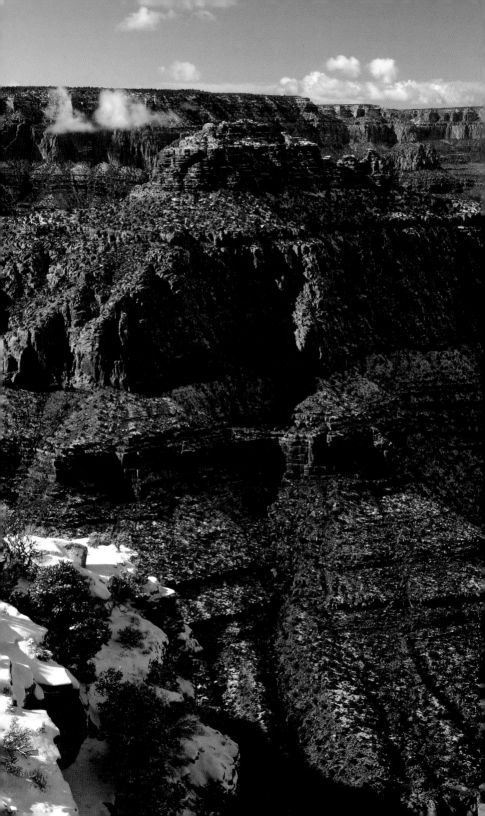

18 MORAN POINT

Moran Point is named after Thomas Moran (above with daughters), one of the most famous and influential landscape painters in the history of American art.

Moran was born in England in 1837, but moved to America with his family in the mid-1800s. At that time, American landscape paintings were drawing blockbuster crowds at art galleries in major cities. Inspired by such works, the young Moran decided to become a landscape painter himself. In 1873 he accepted an invitation from John Wesley Powell to travel to the Grand Canyon. He later wrote of the experience, "it was by far the most awfully grand and impressive scene that I have ever yet seen." A few years later, Moran returned to the Grand Canyon with geologist Clarence Dutton. His works from both of these trips were published in famous books by Powell and Dutton. One of his paintings, "The Grand Chasm of the Colorado," (p.172) hung in the nation's capitol for many years. Deeply moved by his experiences, Moran returned to the canyon every winter between 1899 and 1920. His works provided many people with their first glimpse of the Grand Canyon and helped spur the tourist boom that continues to this day.

Grand Chasm of the Colorado
Thomas Moran, 1873

Large Kiva

19 TUSAYAN RUIN

Tusayan was an Ancestral Puebloan (Anasazi) village that existed here 800 years ago. Its remains were partially excavated in 1930, and today it is the most visited archaeological site in Arizona. There is a 0.1 mile wheelchair accessible path that circles the ruins, which by themselves are not particularly impressive, but a small museum nearby (above) displays exhibits and artifacts that help bring Tusayan to life. Free ranger-guided tours are offered and are highly recommended.

At its peak, Tusayan was probably home to no more than about 30 people. It was one of the last sites the Ancestral Puebloans (p.75) occupied in the Grand Canyon, and it was only occupied for about 20 years—sometime around A.D. 1200. Its main feature was a large 14-room building. Two kivas (ceremonial rooms) were also located nearby. Agriculture provided the majority of the village's food with crops such as corn, beans, and squash grown in a field to the east. Because there is no permanent source of water within seven miles of Tusayan, stone walls were built in the field to retain runoff.

Evidence indicates that health problems were common among Ancestral Puebloans. Chimneys and windows were largely absent from their structures, and smoke-filled rooms contributed to respiratory difficulties. Skeletal remains also reveal teeth worn down to the dentine—the result of eating stone ground cornmeal.

The abandonment of Tusayan and many other Ancestral Puebloans sites in the region is one of the greatest archaeological mysteries in America. For more on this fascinating subject, see page 77.

20 LIPAN POINT

Lipan Point offers one of the most sweeping views on the South Rim. It is also one of the best places to see the rocks of the Grand Canyon Supergroup, which are absent from much of the canyon. These rocks range in age from about 800 million to 1.2 billion years and are easy to identify because they have been tilted at a roughly 20-degree angle (above).

Cardenas Butte, which lies just to the east of Escalente Butte (right), was named in honor of Garcias Lopez de Cardenas, who led a group of Spanish explorers to a spot near Lipan Point in 1540 (p.81).

"Imagine these mountain peaks—hundreds upon hundreds of them—rising one behind the other, stretching away in endless, serried rank until the eye swims and the mind staggers at the task of trying to count them; imagine them splashed and splattered over with all the earthly colors you ever saw and a lot of unearthly colors you never saw before; imagine them carved and fretted and scrolled into all shapes—tabernacles, pyramids, battleships, obelisks, Moorish palaces—the Moorish suggestion is especially pronounced both in coloring and in shapes—mountains, minarets, temples, turrets, castles, spires, domes, tents, tepees, wigwams, shafts."

—Irvin S. Cobb, *Roughing It, Deluxe*, 1913

Escalante Butte

21   DESERT VIEW

Desert View is the final stop on Desert View Drive. At 7,438 feet, it's also one of the highest points on the South Rim. The most prominent feature here is Desert View Watchtower (right), a Mary Colter designed building built in 1932. Colter based her design on the towers found at ancient pueblos in the Four Corners region. A circular staircase leads to the top of the 70-foot tower, the interior of which is decorated with reproductions of Ancestral Puebloan petroglyphs and depictions of Hopi legends. A gift shop is located in the main building.

NOTE: Because Desert View offers the only food and services in the eastern Grand Canyon, it's a good place to fill up on gas (available seasonally) and supplies.

"Days and weeks can be given to Desert View without exhausting the scene or the interest. You are away from the hotel and the crowd, and can see things like a lone eagle from your point of rock . . . the Canyon here is happily disposed for morning and evening effects because it runs practically east and west, and the light strikes not so much across it as along its length . . . One by one the tops of the buttes and points and promontories take up and carry on the light far down the Canyon. First one glows and shifts into a bright garb, and then another farther on repeats the litany of color."

—John C. Van Dyke, *The Grand Canyon of the Colorado*, 1920

Desert View Watchtower

22 BRIGHT ANGEL TRAIL
Recommended

SUMMARY

The Bright Angel Trail is the most popular trail in the Grand Canyon, and with good reason. Descending from the South Rim to the Colorado River, it combines dramatic natural beauty with good footing and convenient facilities. While strenuous, it is a reasonable hike for people of most ages and experience levels.

TRAIL INFORMATION	BRIGHT ANGEL TRAIL

DISTANCE 15.6 miles round-trip   **DIFFICULTY** Strenuous

APPROXIMATE HIKING TIME 2–3 days

TRAIL CONDITION Excellent, maintained

WATER AVAILABILITY Piped in water is seasonally available

ELEVATION CHANGE 4,385 feet

BRIGHT ANGEL TRAIL

0   0.5   MILES   1   1.5

N

PHANTOM
RANCH   23

BRIGHT ANGEL
CAMPGROUND

RIVER TRAIL

PLATEAU
POINT

TONTO TRAIL

DEVILS
CORKSCREW

INDIAN GARDEN
CAMPGROUND

MARICOPA
POINT

YAVAPAI
POINT

THREE MILE
RESTHOUSE

1.5 MILE
RESTHOUSE

BRIGHT ANGEL
LODGE

6

BRIGHT ANGEL TRAIL

DAY HIKES
1.5 Mile Resthouse: 3 miles round-trip
2 Mile Corner: 4 miles round-trip
3 Mile Resthouse: 6 miles round-trip

PARKING
Parking is available in the parking lot a quarter mile south of Maswik Lodge or in the parking area just south of the railroad tracks downhill from Bright Angel Lodge. Parking is also available at Lot E at the Backcountry Office east of Maswik Lodge.

TRAILHEAD
To reach the trailhead, go to the Kolb Studio near Bright Angel Lodge. The trail leaves the rim just to the west of the studio. There is a sign at the trailhead listing such useful information as temperatures, weather forecasts, and sunrise/sunset times.

NOTES
Mules are a common sight on the Bright Angel Trail. Even if you do not encounter a mule train, you will undoubtedly notice their smelly leftovers on the trail.

TRAIL DESCRIPTION
After dropping below the rim, the trail immediately begins to switch back and forth across the canyon walls. There is a small sign detailing the geologic layers you're about to pass through, and one warning you not to hike from the rim to the river and back in one day. This sign, featuring a particularly wretched-looking hiker, is repeated a few times along the trail, and is worth bearing in mind.

The trail, broad and well graded, creeps gently back and forth down the canyon wall. Soon, you'll come to a tunnel blasted through the Kaibab Limestone. Just past this tunnel, a collection of pictographs is visible above you to the left. These ancient drawings are believed to be the work of Havasupai Indians, but they may be the work of an even earlier prehistoric culture.

The view spreading out in front of you is spectacular. Looking down the canyon, you can see the Bright Angel Trail snaking down through the Cottonwood trees that line Garden Creek. Farther along, stark and treeless Plateau Point is clearly bisected by the Plateau Point Trail (p.186).

After the Toroweap formation, you'll pass through a second tunnel. The trail then descends on switchbacks through the tan-colored Coconino sandstone and soon reaches the bright red Hermit Shale. A mile and a half from the start, the trail comes to the creatively named 1.5 Mile Resthouse. This small hut, a good destination for a short day hike, has the same fine overlook as the rest of the trail with bathrooms, seasonal drinking water, an emergency phone, and shade.

A quarter mile past 1.5 Mile Resthouse are some more impressive pictographs. Very easy to miss, they are on the underside of a triangular overhanging boulder 50

Jacobs Ladder

feet above the left of the trail. Red handprints, human figures, and other designs are all visible.

Continuing along the trail, you'll soon reach the sign for 2 Mile Corner—2 miles from the rim and 2.5 miles from Indian Garden. The trail continues to work downward in irregular loops through the red rocks of the Supai Group. The next stop is 3 Mile Resthouse, a hut much like its counterpart but with better views. Water is available here (except in winter), but there are no toilets. There are some small paths behind 3 Mile Resthouse that lead to pleasing and secluded views of the side canyon to the east.

Past 3 Mile Resthouse, the switchbacks grow shorter and shorter. This dramatic section, descending 500 feet through the Redwall formation, is known as Jacob's Ladder. After a series of rapid back-and-forth switchbacks, the trail meets Garden Creek and follows it down toward Indian Gardens.

The trail crosses the creek (which is sometimes dry) just before reaching Indian Gardens, passing by a ranger cabin and small medical station. From here the trail filters downhill through the cottonwoods to the campsites. Each campsite has a roofed picnic table, two boxes to store your food in, and T-Bars to hang your packs on. A bathroom and a water spigot are located a little uphill from the campsites. A spur trail to your left heads to the ranger station and the campsites, where there is a bathroom and water. The main Bright Angel Trail continues straight to the day use area, which also has bathrooms and water. There is a trail from the lower end of the campsite spur trail back to the main trail.

The Bright Angel Trail continues to the right of Garden Creek, while the westbound Tonto Trail (which meets up with the Plateau Point trail) veers off to the left.

Secluded waterfall

Soon, the Bright Angel Trail passes by the pumphouse that brings water to the South Rim. Not long after, it reaches the eastbound junction of the Tonto Trail.

About a mile from Indian Gardens, the creek forms a small but beautiful cascade. Hidden by the narrow canyon that engulfs the creek, the cascade is easy to miss. About three quarters of a mile past the cascade, it is possible to scramble down to the creek and walk upstream to the cascade.

The trail descends to rejoin the level of the creek, crossing it twice. The trail eventually opens out above the imposing Devil's Corkscrew, a twisting 200-foot descent through the Vishnu Schist to the bottom of the canyon. The Devil's Corkscrew loops back and forth across the canyon walls. Although the canyon walls provide some shade, it can be extremely hot in the summer. From the top, the Devil's Corkscrew switches back once and then curls around to the far side of the canyon wall. The trail then zigzags down to rejoin with Garden Creek.

The trail continues along the creek, crossing it twice, and soon reaches River Resthouse, a small hut with an emergency phone. At this point, the Bright Angel Trail officially ends and the River Trail officially begins. Follow the River Trail east as it runs above the Colorado River. After about a mile, the trail reaches Silver Bridge, one of two bridges that span the Colorado near Bright Angel Campground and Phantom Ranch. The second bridge, Black Bridge, lies a short distance upriver and can be reached by continuing along the River Trail. There are some Ancestral Puebloan ruins visible along the path between the two bridges on the north side of the river.

Once across the river, follow the trail to Bright Angel Campground and Phantom Ranch.

Devil's Corkscrew

• PLATEAU POINT •

(3 miles round-trip from Bright Angel Trail)

Plateau Point is one of the most beautiful viewpoints in the Grand Canyon. A trip there is highly recommended if you have enough time.

   The trail to Plateau Point is reached via the Tonto Trail. After crossing Garden Creek just below Indian Gardens, the Tonto Trail heads west and rises slowly as the creek descends to the right. The flat, clear path stays reasonably level as it winds along the contours of the western side of the Garden Creek sub canyon. Another half mile brings you onto the plateau itself, which is completely exposed and shadeless. About three quarters of a mile from Indian Gardens there is a junction with the western branch of the Tonto Trail. Continuing on the Plateau Point Trail, you'll walk across the broad, flat platform for about a mile before reaching Plateau Point. The Point consists of a collection of Tapeats Sandstone slabs overlooking the Colorado River. A railing protects the outermost viewpoints, which provide tremendous views of the Colorado River. The plateau juts out far enough that the views to the east and west stretch on for miles. Sunset, the best time to go to Plateau Point, occurs earlier here than at most rim overlooks, but later than at most other places within the canyon.

Plateau Point

23 PHANTOM RANCH

Phantom Ranch, located at the end of Bright Angel Canyon not far from the Colorado River, offers the only overnight lodging within the canyon. Designed by Mary Colter and built in 1922, this collection of rusic buildings is centered around a main lodge that serves as a restaurant, bar, and general store. Becasue Phantom Ranch is so popular reservations are essential (visitors without reservations will be turned away).

Two types of accomodations are available at Phantom Ranch: private cabins and dormitory-style bunkhouses. Mule riders on overnight trips have first priority for cabins, but if space is available they are rented out to hikers or river runners. The four single-sex dormotories—two for men, two for women—sleep 10 apice, and come with bedding, towels, soap, and showers.

Meals are served family style at the main lodge. Because all food is brought down by mule, meals are expensive and must be reserved in advance. Breakfast costs about $17, pack lunch costs about $10, and dinner costs about $20–$30.

Reservations are handled by Xanterra. They should be booked as far in advance as possible (in the summer, private cabins are booked up to *two years* in advance).

Xanterra Parks and Resorts
PO Box 699
Grand Canyon, AZ 86023
888-297-2757, 303-297-2757
www.grandcanyonlodges.com

Bright Angel Creek

24 SOUTH KAIBAB TRAIL
Recommended

SUMMARY

The South Kaibab Trail is the fastest, most direct route to the Colorado River from the rim. Many overnight hikers choose to descend the South Kaibab Trail, and then return via the less demanding Bright Angel Trail. While most trails in the Grand Canyon follow side canyons, the South Kaibab Trail follows open ridgelines, offering incredible views of the inner Canyon.

TRAIL INFORMATION	SOUTH KAIBAB TRAIL
DISTANCE 13.8 miles round-trip	**DIFFICULTY** Strenuous
APPROXIMATE HIKING TIME 2 days	
TRAIL CONDITION Excellent, maintained	
WATER AVAILABILITY No water	
ELEVATION CHANGE 4,740 feet	

SOUTH KAIBAB TRAIL

DAY HIKES
Ohh-Ahh Point: 1.5 miles round-trip
Cedar Ridge: 3 miles round-trip
Skeleton Point: 6 miles round-trip
Tipoff: 9.2 miles round-trip
Panorama Point: 10 miles round-trip

PARKING
There is no parking near the South Kaibab trailhead. Hikers should take the free Hiker Shuttle or the Hiker Express.

TRAILHEAD
To get to the South Kaibab trailhead, take the free Hiker Shuttle that departs from the Green Line bus stop near the Grand Canyon Information Center. The shuttle will drop you off at the South Kaibab trailhead. There's also the Hiker Express that departs for the South Kaibab trailhead three times a day from the Backcountry Office.

NOTES
While not prohibitively difficult, the South Kaibab Trail has very little shade, no water sources, and no campgrounds between the trailhead and the river. Park rangers do not recommend ascending the trail during the sweltering summer months. While

most of the trail is exposed to the sun during the day, the walls of Yaki Point provide shade until about 10am in the summer for the first mile of the trail.

TRAIL DESCRIPTION

After heading to the right of the information board near the trailhead, you'll immediately drop down into a series of switchbacks running through the pale Kaibab Limestone. Once past the switchbacks, the trail runs gently downhill. The broad path and small walls on the sides of the trail make the steep drop into Pipe Creek Canyon much less intimidating. To the left, pinyon pines scatter across the slope. Bird watchers should keep their eyes out for scrub jays and mountain chickadees.

After a little under a mile the trail reaches Ooh-Ahh Point, a jumble of boulders with broad views across the canyon. Ooh-Ahh Point is a good goal for day hikers who are looking for a quick jaunt into the canyon, but there are even more impressive viewpoints further down the trail. Continuing on, the trail follows some switchbacks before turning the corner around Cedar Ridge and working its way along the crest of the ridgeline toward the Cedar Ridge viewpoint. There are bathrooms and a clearing here. This is one of the best day hike destinations on the trail.

After leading down along Cedar Ridge, the trail wraps around the east side of O'Neil Butte. From here you can see down into the dusty green bowl of Cremation Creek Canyon and the eastern Grand Canyon beyond. After roughly three miles, you leave the ridgeline and walk through a flat landscape dotted with cliffrose, mormon tea, saltbush, and yucca. Soon you'll reach Skeleton Point, an open viewpoint

perched on a precipitous ledge. There is a misleading path to the left that looks like it might be the trail, but the real trail descends to the right and quickly begins to switch back and forth down the steep slope.

Soon, you'll reach a sign indicating that you are 3.8 miles from Bright Angel Campground and 3.5 miles from the trailhead. The switchbacks continue unchanged for another half mile before flattening out. The trail carries on to the north, passes the junctions for both the westbound and eastbound Tonto Trail, and then reaches the rim of the Inner Gorge. This area, known as the Tipoff, is a worthy destination for strong day hikers. Toilets and an emergency phone are located nearby.

Just past the Tipoff, the trail enters its steepest section, dropping roughly 1,600 feet in 1.7 miles. The path swings to the right before curling around and traversing to Panorama Point. Hidden deep in the Canyon, Panorama Point is the most impressive viewpoint on the trail.

Bending back to the right, the South Kaibab Trail drops into the black and pink heart of the Granite Gorge. Descending steadily, the trail loops east and then back west as it approaches a tunnel leading to Black Bridge. Fifty feet above the tunnel, the River Trail (linking the South Kaibab and Bright Angel trails) heads to the west.

The tunnel, blasted through the rock, is dark but short—flashlights or headlamps are not required. After crossing Black Bridge, head west along the north wall. You'll soon see some impressive Anasazi ruins to your left, marking the foundation of a large housing complex. Bright Angel Campground and Phantom Ranch are located farther along the path. If you're planning on spending a full day or two at Phantom Ranch or Bright Angel Campground, the Clear Creek Trail is an excellent day hike.

South Kaibab
suspension bridge

25 HERMIT TRAIL
Highly Recommended

SUMMARY

The Hermit Trail, the Grand Canyon's most popular unmaintained trail, is a rough but worthwhile route from the more remote area west of Grand Canyon Village down to the Colorado River. Reaching the bottom of the Canyon in two steep drops, it's hardly an easy path, but the views and sense of isolation make it one of the best trails in the canyon.

TRAIL INFORMATION	HERMIT TRAIL

DISTANCE 18 miles round-trip   **DIFFICULTY** Strenuous

APPROXIMATE HIKING TIME 2–3 days

TRAIL CONDITION Fair, unmaintained

WATER AVAILABILITY Hermit Creek

ELEVATION CHANGE 4,290 feet

HERMIT TRAIL

N

0   0.5   MILES   1   1.5

HERMIT
RAPIDS

WHITES
BUTTE

TRAVERTINE CANYON

TONTO WEST TRAIL

CATHEDRAL
STAIRS

YUMA
POINT

BREEZY
POINT

EREMITA MESA

HERMIT GORGE

BOUCHER TRAIL

PIMA
POINT

14

HERMITS
REST

HERMIT ROAD

15

SANTA
MARIA
SPRING

DRIPPING SPRINGS TRAIL

HERMIT TRAIL

DAY HIKES
Waldron Trail Junction: 3 miles round-trip
Santa Maria Spring: 4.5 miles round-trip
Dripping Spring: 7 miles round-trip

PARKING
Overnight hikers can park next to the trailhead. Day hikers should park in one of the parking areas near Maswik Lodge or Bright Angel Lodge.

TRAILHEAD
Hermit Road, leading to the trailhead, is closed to the public. If you're camping overnight, however, you can open the gate to Hermit Road with the four-digit access code given to you with your backcountry pass. Drive seven miles to the end of the road, past the paved section, and down a short dirt road to the trailhead. If you're day hiking, take the Red Line shuttle that departs from the Hermit Rest Transfer, located about 200 meters west of the Bright Angel Lodge. You'll pass a number of viewpoints, such as Powell Point, Hopi Point, and the Abyss, which are good stops if you have the time.

NOTES
Parts of the Hermit Trail are fully exposed to the sun in the afternoon. Some hikers cache water on the upper sections of the Hermit Trail for the hike out. No camping is permitted above Hermit Creek Campsite.

TRAIL DESCRIPTION
The Hermit Trail departs from a warning sign on the left side of the parking lot. The Rim Trail's western terminus is also located here. The Hermit Trail runs through the woods at a moderate grade, eventually dropping out from the trees and traversing west for about a quarter mile. At this point the trail descends quite steeply—nearly 1,000 feet over the next mile. Although steep, the trail is well graded and sometimes paved with cobblestones.

As the trail descends, desert plants such as prickly pear cactus and agave start to appear. Three quarters of a mile down (a few switchbacks after the start of the cobblestones) there are some small prehistoric reptile tracks in the sandstone to the left of the trail. Soon after the tracks, the switchbacks become gentler, and the trail re-enters the trees. The Waldron Trail heads off to the left, and this junction is a good goal for many day hikers. The flat, breezy woodlands in this section make a pleasant and shady respite from the open switchbacks. After another quarter mile, the Dripping Springs Trail, another popular day hike, heads west from the main trail.

A half-mile past the Dripping Springs trailhead, you'll reach Santa Maria Springs. The spring itself is only a trickle clinging to the canyon wall, but that trickle runs

into a trough where you can replenish your water if absolutely necessary (the water is slightly foul and should be purified before drinking). Next to the spring is the Santa Maria Springs resthouse, a small three-walled hut with wild canyon grape vines providing shade on the western side.

From Santa Maria Spring the Hermit Trail begins a long traverse through the Supai rock layers. The Supai traverse is dotted with rockfalls. The first few rockfalls, between Santa Maria Spring and the outlooks, are easy to manage, with a beaten path winding through the rocks. However, the rockfalls soon become larger and more difficult to negotiate. Several times you'll have to climb over and around unstable boulders. But patience is more important than strong route-finding skills. Occasionally, there are cairns marking the path of the trail, but don't be surprised to find fresh rockfalls where no trail markers exist.

For three miles past Santa Maria Spring the trail winds in and out with the contours of the land. The trail is nearly flat with sweeping views of the Canyon unfolding below. About a mile past Santa Maria Spring the trail reaches a small, unnamed viewpoint to the left. Continuing on, the trail descends some squiggly switchbacks and opens out onto a larger vista at Lookout Point, an arm of land jutting out about a tenth of a mile from the trail. Lookout Point is a good spot to rest and take in the view. Across Hermit Creek to the west you can see Yuma and Columbus Point.

The trail swings east after Lookout Point, following the curves of the rim as it bears northeast. After another mile, the path swings west to Breezy Point. Once again, the view is excellent, stretching down into Hermit Gorge and the Colorado River beyond. From here it's another half mile to Cathedral Stairs, a precipitous series of switchbacks that drop 500 feet to the desert scrub beneath the Canyon walls. After crossing a particularly tricky rockfall, the trail descends on switchbacks.

Although Cathedral Stairs descends a very steep face, the switchbacks themselves are not too difficult. Cobblestones appear on the trail again, and the trail's surface is generally well put together. Descending a notch between two towers of Redwall, the switchbacks increase in steepness until they reach a flat and gentle section of trail curving around to the northwest. Here the path continues for about a half mile above a talus slope. After Cathedral Stairs, the trail traverses steeply toward its final descent to Hermit Creek. Once past the switchbacks, the trail heads west for half a mile before reaching a junction with the Tonto Trail. The Tonto Trail runs east to west over much of the Grand Canyon below the South Rim. The Hermit Trail then follows the Tonto Trail west (left) to the campsite.

The trail runs three quarters of a mile from the junction to the campsite. A half mile from the junction, there is a good spur trail on the right that takes you straight down to Hermit Creek. Continuing along the main trail, you'll pass the abandoned ruins of the Santa Fe Railroad's Hermit Camp (p.160) before dropping down to the modern Hermit Creek Campsite.

The campsite contains several tent sites spread along and above Hermit Creek. Ammo boxes are provided to protect your food from wild critters. The creek is a good water source, but make sure to filter or purify the water before drinking it. Uphill from the creek is a solar toilet. Down the creek, just past the campsite, is a jewel of a mini-waterfall splashing into a small swimming hole.

The Hermit Trail continues down Hermit Creek for a mile and a half before reaching the Colorado. The trail is very beautiful, but difficult to follow. No longer a defined route, you'll have to pick your way along traces of the trail—some as good as new, some almost gone. The going is rarely tough, however, so you shouldn't have any trouble finding your way. Just follow the creek toward the Colorado.

Following the creek down from the campsite, the walls rise abruptly and soon the wooded creek bed becomes defined by stone slabs. A little farther on, the spur trail running down from the Tonto Trail reaches Hermit Creek. After meandering along, the creek straightens as it descends to the Colorado. A fallen slab soon appears that's as big as a house. At this point, the walls are 150 feet tall, and the trail continues through rocky banks and thickets as it heads toward the river.

Running along the stream, the trail enters a sandy area with some small trees before meeting the Colorado. If you're lucky, you'll catch a glimpse of excited river runners braving Hermit Rapids. Although you can camp by the rapids, the facilities are much better upstream.

If you're staying at Hermit Creek for more than a night, a day hike east along the Tonto Trail is a good option. The trail is very exposed to the sun, but Monument Creek, only two miles from the campsite, is a great destination. This beautiful streambed is relatively easy to follow up and down, but should be avoided if there is any threat of flash flooding.

Trekking through Vishnu Schist

26 GRANDVIEW TRAIL
Highly Recommended

SUMMARY

The Grandview Trail is a steep and beautiful path from Grandview Point to the top of Horseshoe Mesa, one of the few accessible "sky islands" (tree-covered mesas) in the Grand Canyon. The campsite on Horseshoe Mesa is a good destination for a hard day hike, and a good base for exploring the surrounding area. The trail combines the stunning natural beauty of the Grand Canyon with the rich history of its mining days.

TRAIL INFORMATION	GRANDVIEW TRAIL
DISTANCE 6.4 miles round-trip	**DIFFICULTY** Strenuous
APPROXIMATE HIKING TIME 2–3 days	
TRAIL CONDITION Good, maintained	
WATER Hance Creek, Miners Spring, Cottonwood Creek (seasonal)	
ELEVATION CHANGE 1,435 feet	

GRANDVIEW TRAIL

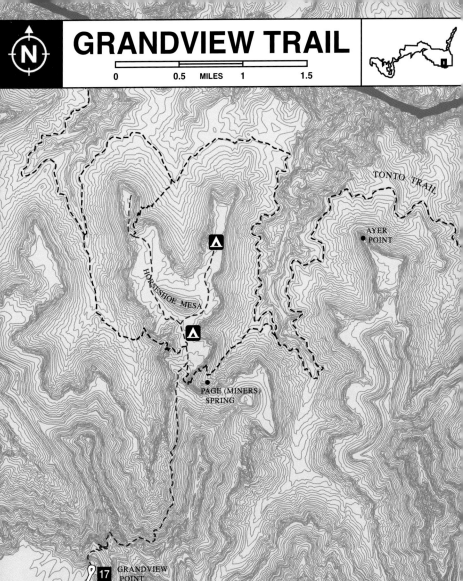

N

0   0.5   MILES   1   1.5

TONTO TRAIL

AYER
POINT

HORSESHOE MESA

PAGE (MINERS)
SPRING

GRANDVIEW
17 POINT

SINKING SHIP

DESERT VIEW DRIVE

GRANDVIEW TRAIL

DAY HIKES
Coconino Saddle: 1.5 miles round-trip

PARKING
There is a parking lot next to the trailhead. The park service prefers that hikers use the upper parking lot at Grandview Point, leaving the lower lot for short-term visitors. Overnight hiker parking is located to the left of the main parking lot as you come in.

TRAILHEAD
To find the trailhead, head east on Desert View Drive away from Grand Canyon Village. After about 10 miles you'll see a sign marking the left turn to Grandview Point. There's a big parking lot with some toilet facilities and an information sign.

NOTES
There are no water sources near the campsite. All water must be brought in. If you hike the trail in the winter, use caution—the first mile of the trail can become particularly dangerous due to snow and ice. There are many abandoned mineshafts on the trial. Do not explore the mineshafts! They have been abandoned for decades and many are extremely dangerous.

TRAIL DESCRIPTION
The trail leaves from the information sign on the right-hand side of Grandview Point. It descends on a series of steep, narrow switchbacks. Although the slope is steep, the footing is usually good as long as the trail is dry. After half a mile the grade becomes a little gentler as the trail zigzags through pinyon pine and juniper. There is a short side trail to the left of the viewpoint that leads out to a small platform with more great views of the Canyon.

The trail turns right at the viewpoint and descends steadily on cobblestones to Coconino Saddle, lying between a rock monolith and the rim. Coconino Saddle is a good destination for a short day hike. From the saddle, the trail traverses to the east,

MINING & TOURISM

As you hike along the Grandview Trail, you'll undoubtedly notice metal cans and other trash left over from the days when Horseshoe Mesa was home to a productive copper mine. The copper mining operation on Horseshoe Mesa, run by Pete Berry, did well until the expense of transporting the ore up to the rim outweighed production costs. Pete Berry ultimately went into tourism and built a hotel at Grandview Point (p.168). The hotel is no longer there, but it was once one of the most popular destinations in the Canyon.

Tonto Platform below Horseshoe Mesa

drops down into the trees, and switches back and forth for several hundred feet. As the trail approaches more open ground, the grade starts to level out. Although the trail is easy to follow, it can be quite rocky and rough.

Soon the trail will pass an old mine shaft, the first of many in the Horseshoe Mesa area. The trail continues past the mineshaft and turns downhill toward Grandview Mesa. As the main trail continues, it crosses a junction with a trail leading to Cottonwood Creek and then passes Pete Berry's old cabin. The small cabin, roofless but still standing, contains some of Berry's old belongings and is worth a quick look. A spur trail near the cabin leads to the small group campsites and a toilet. The large group campsites are located farther down the main trail.

Two short trails run along the sides of Horseshoe Mesa. The shorter trail, which runs to the east, is roughly three quarters of a mile long. It passes through the two group campsites, over a small wash, and then works its way along the Horseshoe Mesa's rim. There are great views of Ayer Point, Miner's Spring Canyon, and the Colorado River to the east.

The second trail runs along the western arm of the plateau. About a mile in length, it swings left below the group campsites, runs west through a small boulder field, and then turns into a stand of junipers. The trail follows a wash for a short distance before becoming a real trail again and heading north. This side of the mesa soon turns into a narrow ridge that widens as the trail continues to the end. Although a route exists at the end that leads down to the Tonto Platform, the steep scramble is not recommended. If you want to visit the Tonto Platform, take the longer route down Cottonwood Creek.

THE
COLORADO

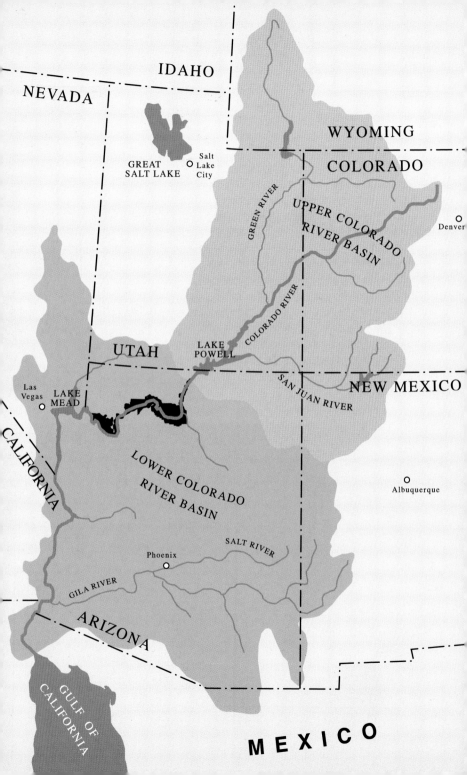

IDAHO

NEVADA

WYOMING

COLORADO

GREAT
SALT LAKE

Salt
Lake
City

GREEN RIVER

UPPER COLORADO
RIVER BASIN

Denver

COLORADO RIVER

UTAH

LAKE
POWELL

NEW MEXICO

SAN JUAN RIVER

Las
Vegas

LAKE
MEAD

CALIFORNIA

LOWER COLORADO
RIVER BASIN

Albuquerque

SALT RIVER

Phoenix

GILA RIVER

ARIZONA

GULF
OF
CALIFORNIA

MEXICO

THE COLORADO RIVER

T HE COLORADO RIVER is the heart and soul of the Grand Canyon. Without it there would be no Grand Canyon, just another quiet stretch of land rolling through northern Arizona. Instead, the river has cut a mile into the surrounding landscape, exposed nearly 2 billion years worth of Earth history, and flushed out over 1,000 cubic miles of eroded debris. The result is the single most impressive natural feature in North America.

As stunning as the view is from the rim, the view on the river is even more spectacular. Upon reaching the Grand Canyon, the Colorado enters one of the most scenic stretches of whitewater in America. Twisting and turning deep into the heart of the canyon, the river exposes a dazzling landscape hidden from much of the outside world. Towering cliffs shelter sandy beaches, dark caverns, and plunging waterfalls. Cool streams trickle down elegant side canyons. Deep shadows mingle with shimmering river light.

Relatively few park visitors get a chance to see the Grand Canyon from the Colorado River. Those who do are filled with an overpowering sense of awe. Visually, it is one of the most dynamic places in the world, changing with the seasons, the weather, and the particular time of day. Even seasoned world travelers admit that a river trip through the Grand Canyon is one of the most remarkable journeys on the planet.

NATURAL HISTORY

F ROM START TO finish, the Colorado River passes through some of the most beautiful and varied terrain in North America. Born in the deep gorges of the upper Rocky Mountains, it plunges head first down the pine-covered slopes to emerge in the desert Southwest. The river cuts through the wind-swept canyons of Utah, tears deep into the Grand Canyon, and then glides through the California desert. By the time it crosses the Mexican border to empty into the Gulf of California, the Colorado has passed through seven western states and drained an area the size of Iraq.

The Colorado River is often referred to as "the Nile of America." At first glance, this comparison seems appropriate. Both rivers pass through vast desert regions and both sustain vast desert civilizations along the way. But despite these two basic similarities, the rivers share little else in common. In terms of size, the Colorado is a much smaller river, draining a quarter of the land that the Nile drains. In terms of length, the Colorado's 1,400 miles pales in comparison to the Nile's 4,000.

Even in America, the Colorado lacks many impressive statistics. It's not the longest river in America. Six other rivers are longer. Nor is it the biggest river in America. In terms of annual flow, the Colorado doesn't even rank in the top 25. But what the Colorado does have, and what makes it so remarkable, is the wildest and most terrifying elevation drop of any river in North America.

From its headwaters in the Rocky Mountains to the Gulf of California, the Colorado drops over 13,000 vertical feet. This steep drop, occurring over a relatively short distance, churns up a river that is fast and furious, dropping an average of 7.7 feet per mile—25 times steeper than the mighty Mississippi. Because a river's erosive power increases exponentially with its speed, the Colorado would be a highly destructive river in any part of the world. But in the desert Southwest, a crumbling landscape filled with soft rocks and sparse vegetation, its erosive power is monumental.

As the Colorado enters the Southwest, it grinds away at the region's barren rocks, picking up tiny particles of sediment along the way. The more sediment the river picks up, the more abrasive it becomes. The more abrasive it becomes, the more

SEDIMENT LOAD

The amount of sediment a river can carry increases to the sixth power of its speed. A river flowing at 2 mph will carry 64 times more sediment ($2^6=64$) than a river flowing at 1 mph ($1^6=1$). Likewise, a river flowing at 10 mph will carry *1 million* times more sediment than a river flowing at 1 mph. During spring floods the virgin Colorado flowed at speeds topping 40 mph, carrying up to 27 million tons of sediment through the Grand Canyon *each day*. During these floods, the Grand Canyon experienced its most intense periods of erosion.

sediment it picks up. This vicious cycle feeds upon itself until the Colorado is, quite literally, a river of liquid sandpaper. Before massive dams plugged the Colorado, the river's sediment loads were phenomenal. Back then the Colorado carried an average of 235,000 tons of sediment through the Grand Canyon *each day*. "Too thick to drink, too thin to plow," was how one early explorer described it. The river's composition was often two parts sediment to one part water, and because the sediment had a high concentration of iron-oxide, the virgin Colorado had a distinct reddish hue.

The virgin Colorado was also psychotically unpredictable. Early explorers often compared it to a bull. It was an "angry bull," a "blooded bull," and a "wild bull of destruction." The Colorado's flows in the Grand Canyon varied anywhere between 3,000 and 200,000 cubic feet per second*, sometimes within a matter of weeks. The largest flows occurred in the spring when snowmelt from the Rocky Mountains set loose months of accumulated precipitation. In any given year, snowmelt accounts for over 70 percent of the river's flow.

The spring floods back then were biblical in proportion. Roaring through the Southwest, they ripped out vegetation, eroded huge chunks of the riverbank, and tumbled 20-ton boulders like ice cubes. During these floods the river carried its heaviest sediment loads, and devoured the landscape at an astonishing rate.

But by winter the Colorado would slow to a trickle and hover just above freezing—a stark contrast to summertime highs that often topped 80 degrees. An entire

---

*A cubic foot per second, cfs, is the standard unit used to measure a river's flow. It refers to how many cubic feet of water a river transports in one second. 1,000 cubic feet of water weighs about 30 tons. In June, when the Colorado was running full force, its flows often topped 100,000 cfs—over 3 million tons of water *per second!*

ecosystem evolved to live in these harrowing conditions. The humpback chub, a fish found only in the Colorado, has a lifecycle timed to these wild temperature swings. It also has strong muscles and an uncanny sense of fluid dynamics to keep from washing away during the spring floods. Plants also adapted to the flooding. Apache plume, mesquite, and catclaw acacia grew only above the flood zone where they wouldn't be washed away.

As it travels to the sea, the Colorado passes through an amazing diversity of landscapes. In the Grand Canyon alone, it encounters three of North America's four deserts. Vegetation typical of the Great Basin Desert, found in Nevada and western Utah, is visible from Lees Ferry to river mile 39. From there, the river enters the northernmost outpost of the Sonoran Desert, covering much of Arizona, Southern California, and northern Mexico. At mile 157 the river enters the Mojave Desert, the smallest of the four deserts but home to such national treasures as Death Valley and Joshua Tree National Parks.

The Colorado River in the Grand Canyon is, on average, 300 feet wide and 25 feet deep. Within the Grand Canyon the river is essentially a series of long pools interrupted by short, quick rapids. Although rapids only account for 10 percent of the Colorado's 277-mile length in the Grand Canyon, they account for nearly half of its 2,000-foot elevation drop. The velocity of water in these rapids is up to 10 times greater than in the long pools in between. On most rivers, rapids form where the riverbed naturally drops, but in the Grand Canyon rapids form next to side canyons. When floods rush through these side canyons, they dump debris into the Colorado. The debris constricts the river, backs it up, and creates a steep dropoff—the rapid. Some of these rapids drop up to 30 feet in a matter of seconds, and the most intense are considered some of the most thrilling whitewater on the planet.

CERTAIN DEATH

IN 1849, an Indian who spoke no English attempted to describe the Colorado River to would-be river runner William Manly. Using a stick to draw in the sand, he mapped the upper Colorado passing through mountains, valleys, and canyons. He then piled up stones to represent the deepest canyon of all. According to Manly, the Indian, "stood with one foot on each side of his river and put his hands on the stones and then raised them as high as he could, making a continued e-e-e-e-e as long as his breath would last, pointed to the canoe and made signs with his hands how it would roll and pitch in the rapids and finally capsize and throw us all out. He then made signs of death to show us that it was a fatal place. I understood perfectly from this that below the valley where we now were was a terrible [canyon], much higher than any we had passed, and the rapids were not navigable with safety."

THE NEW COLORADO

TODAY, THE GRAND Canyon is an oasis of uninterrupted whitewater on a river plugged with dams. Below the Grand Canyon, Hoover Dam holds back Lake Mead, the largest man-made lake in the Western Hemisphere. Above the Grand Canyon, Glen Canyon Dam holds back Lake Powell, the second largest man-made lake in the Western Hemisphere. Almost all of the water that enters the Grand Canyon now passes through the turbines at Glen Canyon Dam, a fact that has significantly altered the downstream ecology.

Since the floodgates at Glen Canyon Dam closed in 1963, the Colorado River in the Grand Canyon has undergone a dramatic transformation. Its flow, temperature, and sediment load—the defining characteristics of the river—have all changed. In fact, other than the path it follows, the new Colorado bears almost no resemblance to the pre-dam river.

The most obvious change has been to the river's flow. Historically, the amount of water flowing through the Grand Canyon was determined by the amount of precipitation that fell on the Colorado River Basin. Today, the amount of water flowing through the Grand Canyon is determined by the engineers at Glen Canyon Dam. Maximum flows are capped at less than 10 percent of what they once were, and the massive spring floods that created much of the Grand Canyon have been eliminated.

This lack of flooding has created several problems. Most notably, much of the debris that is washed into the river through side canyons now lies dormant in the river. Before the dam, spring floods cleared out the debris and washed it downstream. Now the canyon is slowly filling up, and over time the rapids will grow worse and worse.

Although seasonal flows were smoothed out following the completion of Glen Canyon Dam, daily flows became wildly erratic. The amount of water released from the dam is based on the region's fluctuating power demand, and during peak hours in the afternoon, dam operators can charge twice as much for electricity as they can at night. When Glen Canyon Dam first opened, daily flows fluctuated anywhere between 3,000 and 31,500 cfs. Downstream, the river rose and fell like a toilet tank. Daily tides often topped 13 feet and beaches along the banks of the river eroded at an unnaturally high rate. In 1992 the Grand Canyon Protection Act was passed, requiring dam operators to smooth out releases to reduce their ecological impact.

The dam also affects the Colorado's sediment load. Ninety percent of the sediment that used to enter the Grand Canyon is now trapped behind Glen Canyon Dam. Each year Lake Powell fills up with more and more silt, a problem that future generations will have to contend with. In the meantime, water drawn from the clear downstream end of the lake enters the Grand Canyon almost completely silt free.

The water released by Glen Canyon Dam is also drawn from the chilly depths of Lake Powell, entering the Grand Canyon at a constant 45 degrees. Not surprisingly, this frigid water has thrown the river's ecosystem completely out of whack. For millions of years fish native to the Colorado had their life cycles timed to the river's wild temperatures swings. They could survive in cold winter water, but needed warm sum-

DISAPPEARING BEACHES

BEFORE GLEN CANYON Dam was constructed, the banks of the Colorado in the Grand Canyon were lined with hundreds of sandy beaches. These beaches, deposited by the huge sediment loads of the virgin Colorado, provided a valuable habitat for native species and were used as campsites by early river runners. Now that Glen Canyon Dam has reduced the river's sediment load by 80 percent, the beaches have started to erode. Many have disappeared entirely. The erratic releases from Glen Canyon Dam during its first several decades of operation only added to the problem. Timed to coincide with the daily fluctuations in power demand, they created huge tides that stripped sand from the beaches and washed it out of the Grand Canyon.

In 1992 President George Bush signed the Grand Canyon Protection Act. It ordered that Glen Canyon Dam must be operated in a way that protects and enhances Grand Canyon National Park. This included smoothing out the daily releases to limit their ecological impact. As a result, maximum flows are now capped at 26,000 cfs, and daily fluctuations cannot exceed 8,000 cfs.

Scientists were convinced that the smoothed out flows would significantly reduce the erosion of Grand Canyon's beaches. To their dismay, beach erosion

continued at a steady rate. The problem was that any new sediment brought into the Grand Canyon by tributaries—theoretically, enough to replenish the beaches—was languishing at the bottom of the river. What the Grand Canyon really needed, scientists believed, was a flood to stir up the sediment and redeposit it on the riverbank.

In March 1996 Secretary of the Interior Bruce Babbitt turned the wheel at Glen Canyon Dam to release a controlled flood of 45,000 cfs. The flood churned up the river and created more than 50 new beaches. Within a year, however, many of these beaches had disappeared. It turned out that the flood didn't so much create new beaches, as wash existing beaches further downstream. Some scientists have since blamed this failure on the timing of the controlled flood. The tributaries that bring new sediment into the Grand Canyon do so mostly during the rainy summer season. By the spring, when the controlled flood was released, much of this new sediment had already been washed out of the Grand Canyon. If a controlled flood was released at the end of the summer, when the river's sediment loads are at their highest, the beaches might successfully be replenished.

That's the theory at least. Testing it has proved extremely difficult. Every last drop of water in Lake Powell becomes more valuable each year, and many oppose sacrificing this water to test an unproven theory. But something does need to be done before the beaches disappear for good.

mer water to spawn. Now that warm water has disappeared from the Colorado, native fish have been forced to spawn in a handful of smaller tributaries.

As spawning grounds have disappeared, so have the fish. Of the canyon's eight native fish, five are now extinct. Among those lost is the impressive six-foot Colorado squawfish. The humpback chub, one of the few species that remains, has been pushed to the brink of extinction. Scientists estimate that there are fewer than 2,000 humpback chub left. Adding to the problem are non-native sport fish that have been introduced to the river. New arrivals such as trout, catfish, and carp thrive in the chilly water, and compete with the native fish for resources.

But while the new Colorado has devastated native fish populations, it has allowed other life forms to thrive. The cool, clear water allows sunlight to penetrate its depths, fostering the growth of algae. The abundance of algae has formed the foundation of a healthy food chain and turned the river a gorgeous shade of green.

Even the riverbank has undergone a major ecological change. For millions of years the annual spring floods scoured the sides of the river. Now that flooding has been eliminated, a dense thicket of plants has taken up residence in the previous flood zone. This explosion of plants has led to a dramatic increase in animal habitat, and, consequentially, biodiversity.

Glen Canyon Dam completely changed the downstream ecology of the Colorado River. Although many conservationists would like to see the dam destroyed so that the Colorado can be returned to its natural state, Glen Canyon Dam is unlikely to be decommissioned anytime soon. It provides valuable water and electricity to a region that is starved for both. And though the river's ecology has been shaken up, there have been many tangible improvements. The new river supports more plants and animals than the old one ever did, and its regulated flow allows hundreds of river trips to safely navigate the Grand Canyon each year.

HUMAN HISTORY

A LTHOUGH THE COLORADO River is often hard to see from the rim of the Grand Canyon, the canyon itself is clearly visible from space. Equally impressive is the view from space at night when dense clusters of light appear in the surrounding desert. These are the booming cities of the Southwest. Over the past several decades, millions of people have flocked to cities like Phoenix, Tucson, and Las Vegas, eager to leave cold winters elsewhere behind. This phenomenal migration, continuing today, would have been impossible without water from the Colorado River. In a land of little rain, the Colorado is a river of liquid gold that has allowed the Southwest to flourish.

Today, billions of dollars of agriculture, billions of dollars of industry, and millions of daily lives revolve around the Colorado River. Never before in history have so many people and such an enormous economy become so dependent on a single source of water. It is, without question, the most important natural resource in the

West. But it is a limited resource, and huge demands have been placed on it. Today, its flow is so regulated and its water so overused that not a single drop reaches the sea. As the Southwest continues to grow, so do demands on the river. As a result, the Colorado has become one of the most argued over, litigated, politicized, and controversial river in the world.

The first attempt to tap the Colorado was a disaster. In the late 1800s, an enterprising developer named Charles Rockwood realized that, given a steady source of water, the California desert could be turned into an agricultural paradise. If the Colorado River could be tapped and controlled, farmers could grow crops an amazing 12 months of the year.

In 1901 a diversion channel was cut into the Colorado. Overnight, California's previously bone-dry Imperial Valley became one of the most productive farming areas on the planet. But because the Colorado ran thick with sediment, the diversion channel soon silted up and the Colorado jumped its banks, tearing off in a totally new direction. Instead of draining into the Gulf of California, the Colorado flowed into the middle of Southern California. For the next three years the river dumped its entire contents into the desert lowland area known as the Salton Sink. By the time engineers were able to redirect the river, an inland sea roughly one-third the size of Rhode Island had formed. The Salton Sea is still there today.

The Colorado was a force to be reckoned with, but there was too much money at stake to give up trying to tame it. The arid West was on the verge of a massive expansion, and savvy politicians realized that its future was linked directly to its largest river. In the end, there was only one solution: build a massive dam that could regulate the Colorado, hold back its floods, and store them in a reservoir for later use.

In 1933 construction began on Hoover Dam. It was the biggest dam the world had ever seen. It tamed the Colorado, generated an enormous amount of electricity, and allowed the desert to bloom. Hoover Dam was such a resounding success that the government agency responsible for its creation, the Bureau of Reclamation, soon became the golden child of American politics. Using the momentum generated by Hoover Dam, the Bureau set off on a wild tear of dam building that lasted for the next 30 years.

The construction of so many expensive dams created huge economic windfalls in the states where they were built. With so much money at stake, dam building was a politically charged process across the country. But on the Colorado River the issue was even more complex. In 1922 a document called the Colorado River Compact had been drafted to allocate water from the Colorado River to the Colorado River Basin states. The Compact divided the region into an Upper Basin and a Lower Basin, each receiving 7.5 million acre feet of water per year. But it was up to the states to figure out how to divide the water after that.

Not surprisingly, the Compact set off vicious inter-state water wars. Water was essential to each state's growth, and there simply wasn't enough to go around. The only way for a state to secure long-term water rights was to put that water to use before someone else did. The result was the hasty construction of massive multi-billion dollar irrigation projects that, in reality, made little practical sense. In a few short decades 19 dams had been built on the Colorado and its tributaries—many of them poorly conceived—and the river had been sucked dry.

Despite these problems the Bureau of Reclamation continued to push for new dams. In 1963 Glen Canyon Dam was constructed to the furor of conservationists. When two more dams were proposed within the Grand Canyon itself, the conservationists went on the attack. Led by David Brower of the Sierra Club, they used congressional hearings, letter writing campaigns, and modern media savvy to defeat the dams (p.105).

The Bureau's defeat in the Grand Canyon signaled a dramatic shift in popular opinion regarding dams. As the modern conservationist movement took hold, many citizens no longer viewed dams as glorious symbols of progress but as hulking symbols of man's interference with nature. This dramatic shift in public opinion soon brought the era of massive dam building to a halt.

The media blitz that defeated the dams also focused a tremendous amount of attention on the Colorado River in the Grand Canyon. Soon, many ordinary people wanted to see it for themselves. Prior to 1950, fewer than 100 people had paddled through the Grand Canyon. By 1970, 15,000 people were making the trip each year. To limit the river runners' ecological impact, the National Park Service began instituting strict rules and regulations. Today, roughly 20,000 people run the Colorado through the Grand Canyon each year. And while the river as a whole is submerged in controversy, the Grand Canyon remains one of the most rugged and beautiful places in the world.

COLORADO RIVER COMPACT

IN 1922 DELEGATES from seven western states gathered outside Santa Fe, New Mexico, to allocate water from the Colorado River. Their negotiations resulted in the Colorado River Compact. At the time, it was hailed as a "Constitution for the West." In reality, it was one of the most poorly conceived documents in the history of American politics.

The Compact "solved" the issue of water ownership by splitting the Colorado Basin into two: an Upper Basin (Utah, Wyoming, Colorado, New Mexico) and a Lower Basin (California, Arizona, Nevada). Of the estimated 17 million acre feet of water flowing through the Colorado each year, each basin would receive 7.5 million acre feet. Most of the rest went to Mexico. The Compact left it up to the states to decide how the water would be divided up after that. Not surprisingly, the Compact touched off vicious inter-state water wars. Tensions flared and relationships were bruised, but the worst was yet to come.

In 1953, the government admitted that there was a fatal flaw in the Colorado River Compact. The Compact had overestimated the river's annual flow by roughly 3 million acre feet. States that had fought tooth and nail over every last drop of the Colorado River were now faced with the gut wrenching fact that their figures were all wrong. The water rights wars were thrown into turmoil. And they remain in turmoil to this day.

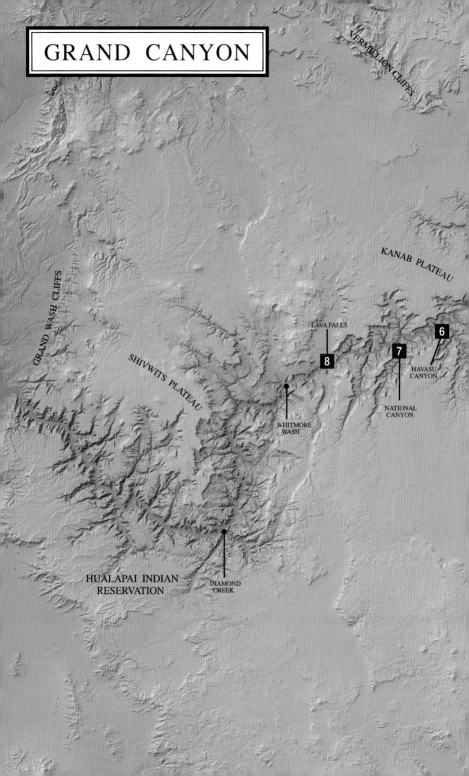

GRAND CANYON

VERMILLION CLIFFS

KANAB PLATEAU

GRAND WASH CLIFFS

SHIVWITS PLATEAU

LAVA FALLS

8

6

7

HAVASU
CANYON

NATIONAL
CANYON

WHITMORE
WASH

HUALAPAI INDIAN
RESERVATION

DIAMOND
CREEK

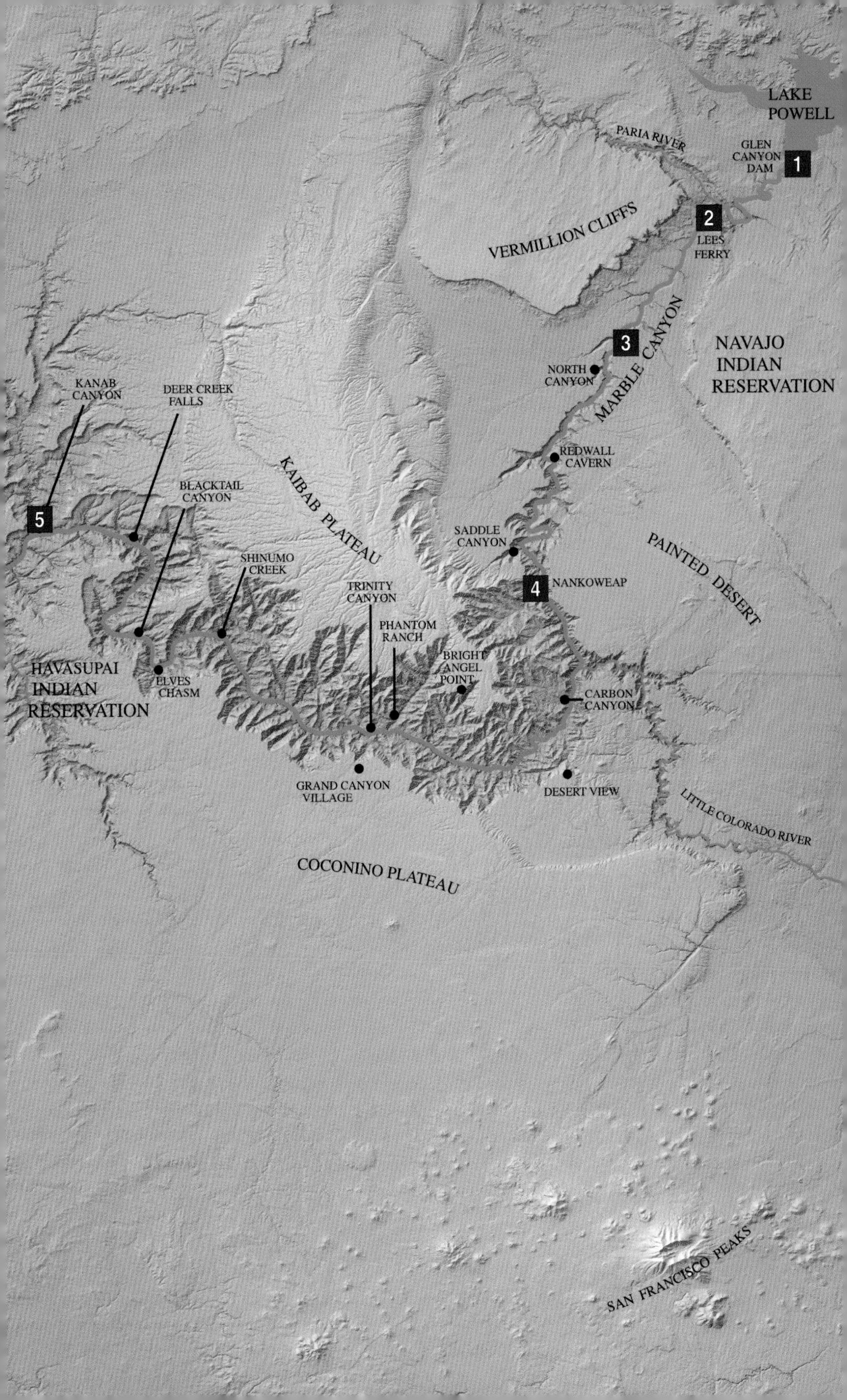

LAKE POWELL
PARIA RIVER
GLEN CANYON DAM
1
2
LEES FERRY
VERMILLION CLIFFS
3
MARBLE CANYON
NAVAJO INDIAN RESERVATION
NORTH CANYON
KANAB CANYON
DEER CREEK FALLS
REDWALL CAVERN
KAIBAB PLATEAU
BLACKTAIL CANYON
5
SADDLE CANYON
PAINTED DESERT
SHINUMO CREEK
4
NANKOWEAP
TRINITY CANYON
PHANTOM RANCH
BRIGHT ANGEL POINT
HAVASUPAI INDIAN RESERVATION
ELVES CHASM
CARBON CANYON
GRAND CANYON VILLAGE
DESERT VIEW
LITTLE COLORADO RIVER
COCONINO PLATEAU
SAN FRANCISCO PEAKS

1 GLEN CANYON DAM

12 miles north of Lees Ferry

Glen Canyon Dam went into operation in 1963. Since then, it has completely changed the characteristics of the Colorado River flowing through the Grand Canyon. Water released from Glen Canyon Dam—drawn from the chilly depths of Lake Powell—enters the Grand Canyon at a constant 47°F. (Pre-dam temperatures often reached 80°F in the summer.) This frigid water has completely altered the downstream ecology of the river (not to mention the bathing habits of most river runners). The dam has also created a river that, unlike the pre-dam Colorado, is remarkably silt-free.

Conservationists hate Glen Canyon Dam. In addition to the changes it has wrought on the Colorado, the dam flooded Glen Canyon, by many accounts one of the most beautiful places in the Southwest. Supporters of the dam claim that Lake Powell is equally beautiful, and the lake allows motorboats to visit previously inaccessible reaches of Glen Canyon. And most importantly, the dam supplies water and power to a region that is starved for both.

Glen Canyon Dam stands 710 feet tall. It took seven years to build and cost $272 million in 1963 dollars. It's 25 feet thick at the crest, 300 feet thick at the base, and contains over 4.9 million cubic yards of cement. If the dam's eight generators operated at full capacity, the dam would release 15 million gallons of water a minute and generate 1.3 million kilowatts of electricity.

For more on Glen Canyon Dam, see page 217.

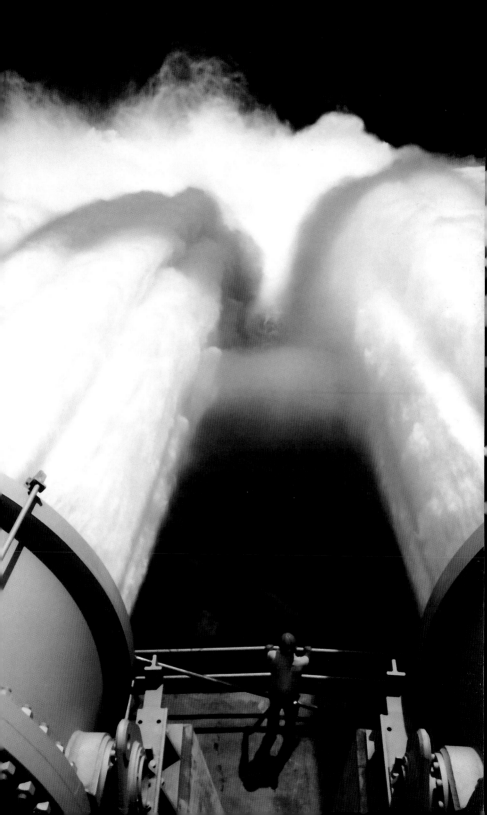

2 LEES FERRY

River Mile 0

Lees Ferry, Arizona (river mile 0) is the official starting point for every Grand Canyon river trip. That's because Lees Ferry is the first place upstream of the Grand Canyon that's accessible by road. (The next stop on the Colorado accessible by road is Diamond Creek, 225 miles downstream.)

Lees Ferry is also the official boundary between the upper and lower Colorado River Basins. That designation was set forth in 1922 by the Colorado River Compact (p.223). The Compact essentially divided the water in the Colorado between Upper Basin states (Utah, Colorado, Wyoming, New Mexico), and Lower Basin states (Arizona, California, Utah). Implementing that deceptively simple plan, however, has proven to be a political nightmare.

In 1776 Fray Velez de Escalante, a Spanish priest who became the first white man to set eyes on Lees Ferry, wrote of this spot, "It has an agreeably confused appearance." Until 1929, when Navajo Bridge was constructed a few miles downstream, the agreeably confused Lees Ferry was the only practical Colorado River crossing for hundreds of miles. John D. Lee (p.93) was well aware of this fact when he established a ferry service here in 1872. Unfortunately, Lee was a convicted criminal on the run from the law, and shortly after he established Lees Ferry he was captured and executed. The ferry service continued to operate until 1928. In that year a ferry carrying a Model T capsized, killing all three people aboard.

3 *MARBLE CANYON*
River Mile 0–61

Marble Canyon gives river runners their first taste of the power and beauty of the Grand Canyon. Its steep, narrow walls offer picturesque scenery broken up by dozens of exciting rapids. Ironically, there's no marble in Marble Canyon. The name was given by John Wesley Powell (p.91), who thought the sedimentary rocks, polished smooth by the muddy river, resembled marble.

In the 1960s, the U.S. Bureau of Reclamation wanted to build a dam at river mile 39. Had the dam been built, the upper reaches of Marble Canyon would have been flooded, but public pressure ultimately defeated the Bureau's plan (p.105).

"We have cut through the sandstones and limestones met in the upper part of the canyon, and through one great bed of marble a thousand feet in thickness. In this, great numbers of caves are hollowed out, and carvings are seen which suggest architectural forms, though on a scale so grand that architectural terms belittle them. As this great bed forms a distinctive feature of the canyon, we call it Marble Canyon."

—John Wesley Powell

Redwall Cavern

Carbon Canyon

Saddle Canyon

4 NANKOWEAP
River Mile 53

Nankoweap is considered by many to be the most beautiful spot in Marble Canyon. In addition to spectacular scenery, it also offers famous archeological sites, pristine camping, and tremendous hiking nearby.

The origin of the name Nankoweap is a bit of a mystery. Some historians claim the word is derived from a Paiute phrase meaning "Place Where Two Tribes Fought." Others trace its origins to a Paiute phrase meaning, "Place That Echoes." What is known is that Nankoweap was home to an Ancestral Puebloan settlement hundreds of years ago. The Ancestral Puebloans (p.75) were an ancient culture that predated Indian tribes such as the Hopi and Navajo. They farmed the fertile delta at Nankoweap and built granaries (stone storage compartments) in the cliffs above.

"And what a world of grandeur is spread before us! Below is the canyon through which the Colorado runs . . . Away to the west are lines of cliffs and ledges of rock—not such ledges as the reader may have seen where they quarryman splits his blocks, but ledges from which the gods might quarry mountains . . ."

—John Wesley Powell

Nankoweap

Trinity Canyon

Shinumo Creek

Granite Gorge

Elves Chasm

Blacktail Canyon

Deer Creek Falls

"The clouds are children of
the heavens, and when they
play among the rocks they lift
them to the region above."

—John Wesley Powell

5 KANAB CANYON
River Mile 143

Kanab Canyon is one of the Grand Canyon's largest and most beautiful side canyons. It was named by John Wesley Powell after the Paiute word for "willow."

Kanab Canyon is where Powell ended his second Colorado River expedition in 1872. Powell and his men hiked out of the canyon and headed to the nearest town. A year earlier, two men had discovered trace amounts of gold in Kanab Canyon, setting off a minor gold rush that brought hundreds of prospectors here. The gold rush lasted all of four months, ending when the prospectors realized there was no more gold to be found.

"The crevices are usually narrow above and, by erosion of the streams, wider below, forming a network of caves, each cave having a narrow, winding skylight up through the rocks. Wherever we look there is but a wilderness of rocks—deep gorges where the rivers are lost below cliffs and towers and pinnacles, and ten thousand strangely carved forms in every direction . . ."

—John Wesley Powell

6 *HAVASU CANYON*
River Mile 157

The beauty of the Grand Canyon is stunning, but the beauty of Havasu Canyon seems almost hallucinatory. This secluded oasis—the most abundant side stream in the Grand Canyon—is part tropical paradise, part Southwestern dreamscape. A well worn path leads up the canyon from the river, revealing shockingly turquoise water tumbling over pink rocks in a series of tranquil pools, each one more beautiful than the last. No matter how far up the path you go, you'll be greeted with some of the most incredible scenery in the country.

Havasu Canyon is located on the Havasupai Indian Reservation. Follow the path up the canyon for 10 miles and you'll reach the village of Supai, home to about 500 Havasupai Indians. (*Havasupai*, loosely translated, means "People of the Blue Green Water.") Supai's world famous waterfalls draw thousands of visitors a year, but the village, located over 2,000 feet below the rim, is only accessible by foot, mule, or helicopter (p.318). It's impossible to hike from the river to Supai and back in a single day, but Beaver Falls, located about four miles up the trail, is a beautiful waterfall that makes a good destination for strong day hikers.

Although Havasu Canyon only receives nine inches of rain a year, it drains a 3,000 square mile basin. That drainage, combined with many springs, provides Havasu Creek with an average of 38 million gallons of water a day. The water is such a lurid blue because the riverbed has a light coating of travertine (calcium carbonate leached from nearby rocks), giving the water an otherworldly hue.

7 *NATIONAL CANYON*

River Mile 166

National Canyon is one of many exquisite side canyons branching off from the Colorado River. These side canyons, carved out over millions of years by flash floods roaring down from the rim, offer some of the most beautiful scenery in the Grand Canyon. Their walls have been sculpted and polished in remarkable ways, catching and concealing the sunlight in an endless variety of patterns. Many of these side canyons are only accessible from the river, making them the exclusive domain of river runners. Some go on for miles, providing incredible day hiking that many river runners consider to be the best part of their trip.

"The gorge is black and narrow below, red and gray and flaring above, with crags and angular projections on the walls, which, cut in many places by side canyons, seem to be a vast wilderness of rocks . . . and ever as we go there is some new pinnacle or tower, some crag or peak, some distant view of the upper plateau, some strangely shaped rock, or some deep, narrow side canyon."

—John Wesley Powell

"What a conflict of water and fire there must have been here! Just imagine a river of molten rock running down into a river of melted snow. What a seething and boiling of the waters; what clouds of steam rolled into the heavens."

—John Wesley Powell

8 LAVA FALLS

River Mile 179

Lava Falls is one of the most challenging, terrifying, and thrilling rapids in the Grand Canyon. It drops 13 feet in a matter of seconds, providing a rip roaring ride regardless of whether you stay inside your boat. Lava Falls also proves that whoever created the Grand Canyon had an excellent sense of drama—it's the last major rapid conquered on most river trips.

Lava Falls is named for the lava flows that have occurred here over the past 2 million years, accounting for the dark-colored basalt on the north side of the river. Roughly 1.6 million years ago, a nearby volcanic eruption sent four cubic miles of lava tumbling down the rim. When the lava cooled it plugged the canyon and formed a dam at least 2,300 feet high. The dam created a reservoir that took 22 years to fill and stretched all the way back to Moab, Utah.

Lava Falls shows mercy to no man, as demonstrated in 1989 when the rapids flipped a boat carrying Hollywood heavyweights Tom Cruise, Jeffrey Katzenberg, and Don Simpson. These Tinseltown titans were on a private "power trip" through the Grand Canyon, popular among movie execs in the late 1980s. The luxury on these trips was so extravagant, so over the top, so beyond *anything* the canyon had ever seen, that they are still talked about to this day. As the moguls conquered the rapids, extra supply rafts tagged along carrying gourmet food, wine, white linens, fine china, assistants, and private chefs. At night, candlelight dinners were served on the banks of the Colorado, featuring delicacies such as caviar, filet mignon, and live lobster.

THE
NORTH RIM

THE
NORTH RIM

LTHOUGH THE NORTH Rim only lies 10 miles away from the South Rim as the crow flies, those of us confined to the ground have to drive 200 miles *around* the Grand Canyon to get there. The closest airport to the North Rim (Las Vegas) is 280 miles to the southwest. As a result, fewer than 10 percent of Grand Canyon visitors ever make it to the North Rim, but those who do are rewarded with a relatively uncrowded scenic paradise. The views are as impressive, if not more, than those on the South Rim.

The North Rim is 1,000 feet higher than the South Rim, resulting in cooler temperatures and 60 percent more precipitation. The higher elevation also means the North Rim is covered in lush forests of spruce, fir, and aspen, giving it a feel more like the Rockies than the desert Southwest. During summer heat spells, when the South Rim is sweltering, the North Rim is greeted with balmy afternoons and mild summer nights. Winters, on the other hand, bring so much snow that AZ-67 (the only road leading to the North Rim) is forced to shut down. Only cross country skiers and showshoers are allowed in the park during this time.

The hub of all activity on the North Rim is Grand Canyon Lodge. Located at the southern end of AZ-67 next to Bright Angel Point, the lodge offers motel-style accomodations right on the rim. More rugged visitors can stay at the pristine North Rim Campground nearby. A drive along Cape Royal Road, which stretches along the Wahalla Plateau, brings you to the spectacular overlooks at Cape Royal and Point Imperial.

The North Rim doesn't have much variety in the way of restaurants or gift shops, but that's all part of its charm. Visitors here are more interested in the rugged scenery and fantastic day hikes through the forests along the rim. Multi-day hikes along the North Kaibab Trail and the exceptionally beautiful—and exceptionally challenging—Thunder River Trail are also popular.

NORTH RIM SIGHTS: p.268-271   **NORTH RIM HIKES: p.272-317**

NORTH RIM

N

0   2   MILES   4   6

GRAND CANYON N.P.

67

POINT IMPERIAL

ROOSEVELT POINT

WIDFORSS TRAIL 7

4

1

3

BRIGHT ANGEL POINT

WALHALLA PLATEAU

2

NORTH KAIBAB TRAIL 9

6 CAPE FINAL

5

CLIFF SPRINGS

CAPE ROYAL

PHANTOM RANCH 23

BRIGHT ANGEL TRAIL 22

24 SOUTH KAIBAB TRAIL

YAVAPAI POINT 3

16 YAKI POINT

SOUTH RIM

64

NORTH RIM
HIGHLIGHTS

Grand Canyon Lodge, p.268
A magnificent lodge
perched right on the rim.

Cape Final Day Hike, p.284
One of the best day hikes
on the North Rim.

North Kaibab Trail, p.296
A fantastic trail that heads to
the bottom of the canyon.

Point Imperial
Sweeping views of the remote
eastern Grand Canyon.

NORTH RIM
HIKING

- **Bright Angel Point, 272 (Easy, 1 mile)**
- **Cape Final. 284 (Easy, 4 miles)**
- **Cliff Spring, 280 (Easy, 1–2 miles)**
- **North Kaibab, 296 (Strenuous, 28 miles)**
- **Powell Plateau, 292 (Moderate, 6–12 miles)**
- **Thunder River , 306 (Very Strenuous, 24–30 miles)**
- **Transept Trail, 276 (Easy, 3 miles)**
- **Widforss, 288 (Easy, 10 miles)**

Bright Angel Point, p.272
Some of the best—and most accessible—views on the North Rim

NORTH RIM
BASICS

IN THE PARK

INFORMATION

The best place to find North Rim information is in the North Rim edition of the park's free newspaper *The Guide*. Copies of *The Guide* are handed out at the park entrance station. The official North Rim Visitor Center is located in the first building to the left of Grand Canyon Lodge. Open daily 8am–6pm. Telephone: 928-638-7864

GETTING TO THE NORTH RIM

There's only one road to the North Rim: AZ-67, which heads south from the small town of Jacob Lake off I-89A. From Jacob Lake follow AZ-67 south for 44 miles to reach the Grand Canyon Lodge. No buses or trains run to the North Rim, but there is a transcanyon shuttle between the North and South Rim (see below). The closest major airports are located in Las Vegas, Nevada, and Salt Lake City, Utah. Las Vegas is the closer city, located 280 miles away. Salt Lake City is located 380 miles away.

RIM TO RIM SHUTTLE

From mid-May through mid-October, a daily shuttle runs between the North and South Rims. The shuttle leaves the North Rim at 7am and arrives at the South Rim by noon. It leaves the South Rim at 1:30pm and arrives at the North Rim by 6:30pm. Cost is $65 one-way, $110 round-trip. Reservations are necessary. Telephone: 928-638-2820

WHEN TO GO

Summer is the busiest time on the North Rim, but the crowds never come close to those found on the South Rim. Fall brings changing leaves and limited crowds, making it one of the best times to visit. In the winter, the road to the North Rim is closed due to snow. During this time (about mid-May to November) all facilities on the North Rim are closed, but the park remains open to snowshoers and cross country skiers. Spring brings fewer crowds, but temperatures can stay chilly until June.

FEES

The entrance fee for the North Rim (which also gives you access to the South Rim) costs $20 per vehicle or $10 per pedestrian, motorcycle rider, or cyclist. Admission is good for seven days. Another option is to purchase a National Parks Pass (also available at the entrance station) for $50 that gives you unlimited access to all U.S. national parks and national monuments for one full year.

WEATHER

Because of its higher elevation the North Rim is about 5–10 degrees cooler than the South Rim. The North Rim also receives significantly more precipitation—in the winter, snowfall can top 10 feet. Late summer (monsoon season) often brings short afternoon thundershowers.

WHAT TO BRING

Clothes: Warm clothes and rain gear are essential at any time of the year. Supplies: Plan on bringing anything you need that you wouldn't be able to buy at a typical convenience store back home. Although there's a general store on the North Rim, its selection of food and supplies is limited.

NORTH RIM CLIMATE

(Figures based on annual averages)

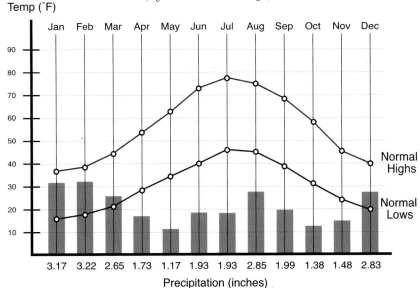

LODGING

GRAND CANYON LODGE

Grand Canyon Lodge offers the only in-park lodging on the North Rim. There are four types of rooms available, all with telephones:

Frontier Cabins: $92+ per night
One double bed, one single bed, 3/4 bath.

Pioneer Cabins: $101+ per night
Two bedrooms separated by 3/4 bath. One double bed, three single beds.

Western Cabins: $106+ per night
Two queen beds, full bathroom, porch. Four Western Cabins offer rim views, but these cabins are booked as much as two years in advance.

Motel Rooms: $91+ per night
One queen bed, full bath.

Rooms are often booked months in advance during the summer, but same day reservations are sometimes available. Open from mid-May to mid-October.

Telephone: 303-297-2757, 888-297-2757
www.grandcanyonnorthrim.com

CAMPING

NORTH RIM CAMPGROUND

The North Rim Campground is located in a ponderosa forest about a mile northwest of Grand Canyon Lodge. The Transept Trail (p.276) runs between the campground and the lodge. There are 87 sites (no hookups), four with views of the canyon. Regular sites cost $15 per night; the four sites with views cost $20 per night. Backpackers and other visitors without cars only pay $4 per night. Reservations are available and are highly recommended.

Reservations: 800-365-2267; same day 928-638-2611
www.reservations.nps.gov

GETTING AROUND

BY CAR

If you plan on venturing away from the Grand Canyon Lodge area (that is, along Point Imperial Road or Cape Royal Road), having your own car is essential. Other than the Hiker Shuttle to the North Kaibab Trailhead, there's no public transportation on the North Rim.

BY SHUTTLE

The only local shuttle service on the North Rim is the Hiker Shuttle that runs between Grand Canyon Lodge and the North Kaibab trailhead. Cost is $5 for the first person, $2 for each additional person. Departs 5:20am and 7:20am daily. Purchase tickets at the front desk of the Grand Canyon Lodge.

ON FOOT

There are several trails and overlooks within walking distance of the Grand Canyon Lodge complex. Exploring the rest of the North Rim on foot is not practical.

BY BIKE

Bikes are allowed on all paved and dirt roads on the North Rim unless otherwise posted. They are prohibited on all other park trails. Bicyclists must obey all traffic regulations. If you want to explore the North Rim via bike, you'll have to bring your own. There are no bike rentals on the North Rim.

DINING

GRAND CANYON LODGE DINING ROOM

The finest dining on the North Rim. Classic American fare with tremendous views of the canyon. Entrees run $15–24. Open for breakfast (6:30–10am), lunch (11:30am–2:30pm), and dinner (4:45–9:30pm). Dinner reservations are required, and should be booked well in advance.

Telephone: 928-638-2612 ext. 160

CAFE ON THE RIM

Cafeteria-style fast food. Located on the west side of the Grand Canyon Lodge complex. Open 7am–9pm.

ROUGH RIDER SALOON

Coffee shop by day, well stocked bar by night. Located on the east side of the Grand Canyon Lodge complex. Open 5–9am, 11am–10pm.

SERVICES

NORTH RIM GENERAL STORE

Located at the entrance to the North Rim Campground. Offers basic groceries and camping supplies. Open 8am–8pm, but hours sometimes vary with demand.

GAS

Located on the road leading to the North Rim Campground. Open 7am–7pm daily.

SERVICES (continued)

POST OFFICE

Located in the Grand Canyon Lodge. Window service Monday through Friday 8–11am & 11:30am–4pm; Saturday 8am–1pm.

LAUNDRY & SHOWERS

Coin-operated laundry and showers are located just outside the North Rim Campground entrance. Open 7am–7pm daily.

ENTERTAINMENT

RANGER PROGRAMS

The park offers a variety of free ranger programs that are highly recommended. Topics cover a wide range of subjects including history, geology, wildlife, and more. Check *The Guide* or stop by the Visitor Center for topics and times.

MULE TRIPS

Mule trips are offered daily on the North Rim. Only day trips are offered—there are no overnight rides. A one-hour ride along the rim costs $30. A half-day trip along the rim or inner canyon costs $55. Full-day trips follow the North Kaibab Trail (p.296) to Roaring Springs and cost $105 (includes lunch). Register at the Grand Canyon Trail Rides desk in the lobby of Grand Canyon Lodge. Open 7am–5pm daily.

Telephone: 435-679-8665

OUTSIDE THE PARK

JACOB LAKE & AZ-67

There are only a handful of shops and establishments in the tiny town of Jacob Lake, and only a handful more along AZ-67. The only restaurants are located at the Jacob Lake Inn and the Kaibab Lodge. When snow closes AZ-67, all establishments except the Jacob Lake Inn close until the following spring.

KAIBAB PLATEAU VISITOR CENTER

Offers exhibits and information on the surrounding area. Located near the junction of 89-A and AZ-67. Open 8am–5pm daily.

Telephone: 928-643-7298

LODGING (Jacob Lake & AZ-67)

JACOB LAKE INN

Offers motel rooms, cabins, and family units that sleep up to six. Open year-round.
Rates: motel rooms, $96+; cabins, $76+; family units, $126+
Telephone: 928-643-7232
www.jacoblake.com

KAIBAB LODGE

Offers rustic cabins that sleep up to six. Located 26 miles south of Jacob Lake.
Rates: $80+ per night
Telephone: 928-638-2389, 800-525-0924
www.canyoneers.com

CAMPING (Jacob Lake & AZ-67)

DEMOTTE PARK CAMPGROUND

Located next to Kaibab Lodge. Open June through late September. $10 per vehicle
per night. No reservations.
Telephone: 928-638-2389, 800-525-0924
www.canyoneers.com

JACOB LAKE CAMPGROUND

Offers camping sites for $10 per vehicle per night (tent camping only). Located just
west of 89-A/AZ-67 junction. Open mid-May to October. No reservations.
Telephone: 928-643-7770

KAIBAB CAMPER VILLAGE

Offers tent and RV sites for $12 per night ($22 per night for sites with RV hookups).
Open mid-May to mid-October. Reservations are available.
Telephone: 928-643-7804, 800-525-0924

SERVICES (Jacob Lake & AZ-67)

NORTH RIM COUNTRY STORE

Offers gas, groceries, camping, and auto supplies. Located across the highway
from the Kaibab Lodge.

JACOB LAKE INN GAS STATION & STORE

Offers gas and basic groceries. Located next to Jacob Lake Inn.

1 GRAND CANYON LODGE

Shortly after the creation of Grand Canyon National Park, Steven Mather, the director of the National Park Service, urged the Union Pacific Railroad to build a number of grand lodges in several western parks. And so, in 1928, construction began on Grand Canyon Lodge on the North Rim. Designed by Gilbert Stanley Underwood, who also designed Yosemite's Ahwahnee Hotel, the original lodge was built out of native ponderosa pines and Kaibab limestone. But just four years after it opened, a fire burned down the original building. (Fortunately, the small cabins on either side of the lodge were spared and are still used by guests today.) The current lodge was built in 1936. When it was finished, it boasted such improvements as steel beams—instead of flammable pine beams—and sloped roofs to deflect the heavy snows.

Grand Canyon Lodge should be the first stop for every North Rim visitor. Perched right on the edge of the canyon, it offers some of the best views in the park. The open air terraces on either side of the lodge are a great place to relax on a sunny day. (At night, a fire is often built in the stone fireplace on the eastern terrace.) Sandwiched between the terraces is the indoor Sun Room, where leather chairs face giant picture windows, creating the most comfortable views on the North Rim. Finally, there's the Grand Canyon Lodge Dining Room, where several tables are located next to the large windows on the southern wall. The views are tremendous, but these popular tables are assigned at random.

Point Imperial

2 WALHALLA PLATEAU

The Walhalla Plateau is a 15-mile peninsula of land jutting out into the canyon just east of Bright Angel Point. It contains some of the North Rim's finest viewpoints, and the only ones accessible by car other than those near Grand Canyon Lodge. The Walhalla Plateau can be reached via Fuller Canyon Road, which heads east off AZ-67 three miles north of Grand Canyon Lodge. Soon the road reaches a fork—heading left takes you to Point Imperial, heading right takes you to Cape Royal.

Head left and you'll drive about three miles along Point Imperial Road before reaching Point Imperial. At 8,803 feet, Point Imperial is the highest vantage point on either rim. The impressive spire to the east marks the top of Mount Hayden.

Head right at the junction and you'll follow Cape Royal Road toward Cape Royal, 16 miles south. Along the way you'll pass by a number of worthwhile viewpoints including Vista Encantada (which has picnic tables) and Roosevelt Point (which provides a rare glimpse of the confluence of the Colorado River and Little Colorado River). Cape Final (p.284) is a short, highly recommended day hike that starts six miles past Roosevelt Point. Continuing along Cape Royal Road you'll reach Walhalla Overlook. Across the road from the overlook are the remains of a six-room Anasazi pueblo, thought to have been inhabited around A.D. 1050.

At the end of Cape Royal Road is a large parking area. A short, paved path leads from the parking area to Cape Royal, the southernmost viewpoint on the North Rim. It provides almost full, 360-degree views of the canyon. Along the way you'll pass Angels Window, a natural archway that frames a view of the Colorado River.

Cape Royal

3 BRIGHT ANGEL POINT

Recommended

SUMMARY

The paved path to Bight Angel Point is an easy, accessible introduction to the awe-inspiring views of the North Rim. It is broad and smooth all the way to its spectacular lookout. The Bright Angel Trail is suitable for nearly every visitor.

TRAIL INFORMATION	BRIGHT ANGEL POINT

DISTANCE 1 mile round-trip   **DIFFICULTY** Easy

APPROXIMATE HIKING TIME 15 minutes

TRAIL CONDITION Good, paved

WATER AVAILABILITY No water

ELEVATION CHANGE 90 feet

BRIGHT ANGEL POINT

PARKING
There is a large parking lot just north of Grand Canyon Lodge.

TRAILHEAD
The path to Bright Angel Point begins to the left of the North Rim Visitor Center, just beyond the cabin area. The trailhead is the highest point on the trail and the path slopes downward immediately after you pass through some nearby fencing.

TRAIL DESCRIPTION
The path to Bright Angel Point is entirely paved, making it more like a sidewalk than an off-road trail. After the initial drop at the start, the trail stays relatively flat with only a few mild ups and downs. Dramatic views of Roaring Springs Canyon unfold to your left. On your right is Transept Canyon, but clear views of it are blocked for much of the trail.

Towards the end of the trail you will come to a small bridge that takes you to Bright Angel Point. A metal railing surrounds Bright Angel Point, and on a nice summer day you will be joined by plenty of other people taking in the outstanding view.

The physical features visible from Bright Angel Point are almost too numerous to count. Stretching out in front of you is Bright Angel Canyon, home to the North Kaibab Trail that descends all the way to the Colorado River. In the middle of the foreground, Deva, Brahma, and Zoroaster Temples rise out of the depths of the canyon. To the right are Buddha and Manu Temples. Closer in is Oza Butte. The South Rim appears as a sheer wall on the far side of the canyon. Farther out, past the South Rim, are the San Francisco Mountains including Kendrick, Silgreaves, Bill Williams, and Humphrey's Peaks. At 12,643 feet, Humphrey's Peak is the highest point in Arizona.

The rocky outcrop directly behind the observation platform is a popular place to grab a seat and take in the view. If you do choose to climb onto this overlook be extremely careful of the sheer drops down the sides.

WHITE-THROATED SWIFTS

White-throated swifts are a common sight at Bright Angel Point in the summer. These aptly named birds swoop to and fro at astonishing speeds, producing a loud whirring sound that alternately delights and alarms people taking in the view. Swifts build their nests on high canyon cliffs. As a result, they are difficult to study, and much about their behavior remains unknown. Although there are roughly 100 species of swifts worldwide, only four are found in North America. In Asia, the nest of one species of swift is aggressively harvested for use in bird's nest soup.

4 *TRANSEPT TRAIL*

SUMMARY

The Transept Trail, a charming nature walk along the edge of Transept Canyon, offers an easy stroll combined with some great views. The trail makes for a pleasant morning or evening hike with frequent wildlife sightings.

TRAIL INFORMATION	TRANSEPT TRAIL
DISTANCE 3 miles round-trip	**DIFFICULTY** Easy
APPROXIMATE HIKING TIME 1.5 hours	
TRAIL CONDITION Good, maintained	
WATER AVAILABILITY No water	
ELEVATION CHANGE 100 feet	

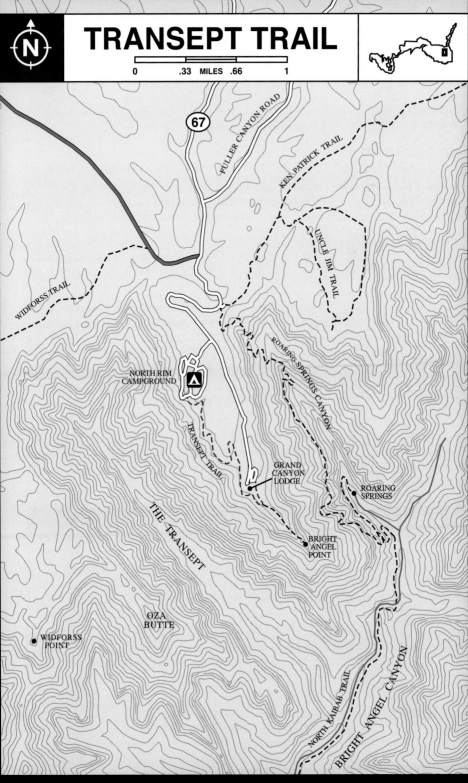

TRANSEPT TRAIL

PARKING
Parking is available at the North Rim Campground.

TRAILHEAD
The Transept Trail runs between the North Rim Campground and the Grand Canyon Lodge. The campground trailhead is found just west of the general store. There is a sign marking the trail. (To follow the trail from Grand Canyon Lodge, start the Bright Angel Point Trail and turn right off of the pavement after a tenth of a mile.)

TRAIL DESCRIPTION
From the campground: The trail is broad and flat as it leaves the campground. For the first third of a mile, the campground and its accompanying fields remain visible through the trees on the left. Soon, several fine viewpoints appear on the right. The trail's namesake, the Transept, is the massive rock outcrop on the opposite side of Transept Canyon, which drops down to the right of the trail. The Transept is distinguished by its pale top layer and red brick bottom. Beyond Transept Canyon you can see Brahma, Deva, and Zoroaster Temples in the main body of Grand Canyon.

As the trail continues, you'll see several small side trails that lead out and back from the main trail. These trails are rugged and unmaintained and some lead to dangerous viewpoints. If you choose to explore the side trails, use caution.

As the main trail continues, it turns left into a tangled woody grove. It dips down slightly before cutting right and returning to the rim. The trail then follows the contours of the nearby streambeds, sometimes crossing over them on small bridges. This pretty section of the trail is filled with ponderosa pines and aspens that contrast well with the dramatic canyon views.

KAIBAB SQUIRREL

The Kaibab squirrel is one of the most fascinating creatures in the Grand Canyon. Found only in the ponderosa pine forests of the North Rim, it is completely dependent on ponderosas as a source of food. Distinguished by its flamboyant white tail and dark grey body, the Kaibab squirrel is closely related to the Abert squirrel found on the South Rim. Although the two squirrels share a common ancestor, they became geographically isolated when the ponderosa forests retreated to the high rims of the Grand Canyon at the end of the last Ice Age. After thousands of years of evolution, the Kaibab squirrel developed its own unique physical characteristics, most notably its distinguished white tail.

Wildlife is a common sight on the Transept Trail. Among the most frequently spotted animals are mule deer, chipmunks, and squirrels. Birdwatchers should keep an eye out for wrens, juncos, and woodpeckers. The density of animals here is the result of the trail's close proximity to both the campground and the lodge. The animals are drawn to the food that people accidentally leave behind. Note: You should never intentionally feed the animals. If they grow dependant on summer visitors the winter will be a hungry time for them. Feeding animals is also illegal—rangers will ticket you.

As the trail continues, it passes the foundation of an ancient Anasazi structure. Although not very large, it still survives despite the passing of the centuries. Shortly after the ruins, the trail veers left toward a large outlook on a little shoulder of land. Benches are set up here from which you can see Bright Angel Point, Bright Angel Canyon, and the Temples beyond. Farther down the trail you may see several burnt-out trees. As with many North Rim trails, the Transept was swept by fire and retains some damage.

The trail gradually rises back toward the rim, passing the cabins of the Grand Canyon Lodge on the left. Eventually, the trail leads back to the lodge itself. There are more outlooks to your right, several of which stretch out on precipitous tongues of rock. The trail continues through shaded stretches of tall trees and sunny open sections, eventually passing by the front of the lodge. The trail ultimately merges with the pavement of the Bright Angel Point Trail.

5 CLIFF SPRING TRAIL

SUMMARY

Cliff Spring brings the hiker through an ancient woodland glade to a peaceful spring. While not particularly challenging, the trail does have some marked rises and falls, as well as some steep drop offs if the path is followed to the end.

TRAIL INFORMATION	CLIFF SPRINGS TRAIL

DISTANCE 1–2 miles round-trip   **DIFFICULTY** Easy

APPROXIMATE HIKING TIME Up to 1 hour

TRAIL CONDITION Good, unmaintained

WATER AVAILABILITY Cliff Spring, requires treatment

ELEVATION CHANGE 200 feet

CLIFF SPRING

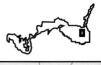

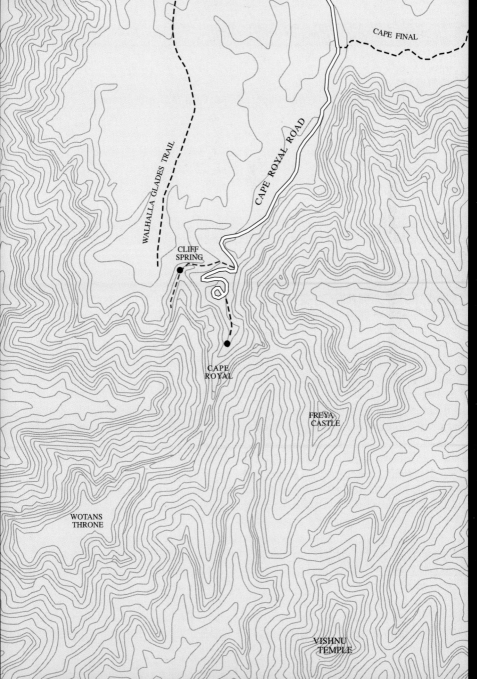

CAPE FINAL

WALHALLA GLADES TRAIL

CAPE ROYAL ROAD

CLIFF
SPRING

CAPE
ROYAL

FREYA
CASTLE

WOTANS
THRONE

VISHNU
TEMPLE

CLIFF SPRING TRAIL

PARKING
There is a parking area across the street from the Cliff Spring trailhead.

NOTES
Because Cliff Spring is one of the few consistent water sources on the North Rim, it is an excellent spot for bird watching.

TRAILHEAD
The Cliff Spring Trail starts inside of a hairpin right-hand turn a half mile from the end of Cape Royal Road (13.7 miles south of the junction with Point Imperial Road). Parking is available at a pullover on the left side of the road. There is a signed trailhead across the street. The well-maintained dirt trail drops down from the road into a forest of ponderosa pines. Watch out for thistles by the side of the path.

TRAIL DESCRIPTION
The Cliff Spring Trail has been used since ancient times. Shortly after the trailhead there is an Ancestral Puebloan granary to your right. The structure, well built of limestone and held together with a basic mortar, speaks highly for the ingenuity and craftsmanship of the Ancestral Puebloans. Granaries such as this one were constructed to store crops such as beans, corn, and squash.

The trail continues to slope downward, running parallel to a creek bed on the left before crossing over it. It curves around a large boulder and through a pleasant mini-valley before re-crossing the creek. As the trail continues, it hugs some striking 30-foot cliffs to the right. The cliffs have a pronounced overhang that makes for an interesting hike. Soon the cliffs back off a little and some small cacti start to appear. The trail bends to the right and flattens out next to the plummeting creek bed, where what was a dip suddenly becomes its own narrow canyon. The Cliff Spring Trail continues above the tops of evergreen trees, sheltered in the side of a pale sandstone wall. The trail is about 20 feet wide at this point.

Soon, the small clumps of vegetation clinging to the canyon walls become thick and mossy. Fern-like thistles spring up to the right. There is a dripping sound here, and you can see Cliff Spring squeezing itself out of the rock. Because this is a constant source of water, it is an excellent place for bird watching. Violet-green swallows, rock wrens, and ravens all nest nearby. There is a large flat rock from which you can gaze out into the depths of the canyon and revel in this unique space lying 500 feet below the rim. In the distance you can see Wotan's Throne rising perpendicular to Cape Royal and Cliff Spring.

Cliff Spring

The cliff marks the end of the maintained Cliff Springs Trail, but a rugged path continues a half mile farther. The trail curls left toward the southernmost tip of the Wallhalla Plateau. This unofficial trail leads straight from the spring and turns sharply left after a tenth of a mile. The awning-style overhang lowers, the trail narrows, and the footing becomes more rugged. The small dirt path leads past plants such as agave, Mormon tea, and Utah serviceberry before hugging the cliff again. The overhang is now low enough that you will probably have to duck to squeeze through it. This part ends quickly, however, and the rugged path soon continues. Cape Royal appears on the left across the canyon. The going here is quite rough, but the trail is easy to see. A quarter mile from the spring, the trail looks as if it might climb up a steep slope to a saddle in the cliff, but it doesn't. Instead, the route continues to hug the cliff face, but remains separate enough that the gigantic rock and boulder formations are easily visible overhead. Curling around the end of Wallhalla Plateau, the trail heads closer to the cliffs, slopes down a little, and ends in a flat section of red sandstone. From here you can retrace your steps back to Cliff Spring.

View more photos online!
www.destinationpress.com

6   *CAPE FINAL TRAIL*

Highly Recommended

SUMMARY

The Cape Final Trail runs through cool open woodlands to a dramatic and uncrowded eastern vista. A spectacular day hike, this trail is also an excellent short camping trip, and can be accomplished by almost anyone able to carry a backpack.

TRAIL INFORMATION	CAPE FINAL TRAIL

DISTANCE 4 miles round-trip   **DIFFICULTY** Easy

APPROXIMATE HIKING TIME 2 hours

TRAIL CONDITION Good, rehabilitated dirt road

WATER AVAILABILITY No water

ELEVATION CHANGE 150 feet

CAPE FINAL

0   .5   MILES   1   1.5

GUNTHER
CASTLE

FRANCOIS MATTHES TRAIL

CAPE ROYAL ROAD

SIEGFRIE
PYRE

NAJI
POINT

NATCHI CANYON

WALHALLA GLADES TRAIL

JUNO
TEMPLE

CAPE
FINAL

JUPITER
TEMPLE

VENUS
TEMPLE

CAPE
ROYAL

APOLLO
TEMPLE

FREYA
CASTLE

BASALT CLIFFS

WOTANS
THRONE

VISHNU
TEMPLE

KRISHNA
SHRINE

RAMA
SHRINE

CAPE FINAL TRAIL

PARKING
There is a parking area next to the trailhead.

TRAILHEAD
From Grand Canyon Lodge, drive north on AZ-67 and turn right on Cape Royal/Point Imperial Road. Drive 5.4 miles until you reach a "Y" junction. Bear right toward Cape Royal. After about 15 miles, a sandy parking area will appear on your left. The trail leads to the left of the parking area into the stately forest of ponderosa pines.

NOTES
It is possible to camp at Cape Final. The Backcountry Office gives out one camping permit per night, so if you have one, you will have Cape Final all to yourself! Cape Final itself can be a bit hard to find. Look for USGS datum points embedded in the bedrock at the overlook.

TRAIL DESCRIPTION
The trail rises slightly at the start with the land sloping down a little on either side. The trail is dirt with a few rocks, but flat and broad enough for two people with backpacks to walk shoulder to shoulder. Pay no attention to the occasional diamond-shaped pieces of tin nailed to trees. They were once used as trail markers when snow covered the trail, but at present they are disused and unnecessary.

As you walk, the edge on your right-hand side begins to come closer. Soon, you can catch a glimpse of the canyon's rim to your right through the trees. After another half mile the upward grade ends and the trail flattens out of its gentle climb, curving gradually to the right and undulating a bit up and down. As you meander through the pines, the land on either side begins to narrow. Eventually you will cross a small creek bed. The trail continues for another mile as you approach the edge of the woods.

At this point a small side trail goes left to the first overlook, a dramatic drop to the east. The overlook's sudden red emptiness comes as a wonder and a shock after walking through the forest. From here the trail narrows but remains good, rolling along parallel to the spit of land that you're following. There is another equally impressive viewpoint a short distance later. The trail then turns to the right and winds through the woods as the peninsula you're on grows narrower and narrower.

Continuing along, the trail plunges left into the scrub and the vegetation begins to get a little more desert-like as cacti and pinyon pines replace ponderosas. The trail drops sharply for 50 feet, then returns to its normal flat grade. Soon you'll reach the clearly marked Cape Final side trail. This trail winds through low cacti and scrub (climbing some white rocks that may require your hands to steady you) before opening out onto a spectacular view of the eastern canyon.

In front of you, Jupiter Temple and Juno Temple rise in a fin-like ridge. To the

left, you can see the towering Siegfried Pyre, with Hubbell Butte and Chiavria Point extending from it to the south. To your right, you see the pyramids of Vishnu Temple and Rama Shrine, with Krishna Shrine just in sight to the far right. The Unkar Creek bed runs between you and Jupiter Temple, winding around to the east of Rama Shrine before passing out of sight. Behind Jupiter and Juno Temples you can see the black of Lava Butte and Chuar Lava Hill. North of them is Temple Butte. Beyond it all are the walls of the South Rim.

After Cape Final, the trail narrows again but remains easy to follow. Along the way it passes a number of other outlooks to the left. The trail ultimately peters out at a southern outlook from which you can see Freya Castle off to the right.

CAMPING

The Backcountry Office only gives out one camping permit to Cape Final per night, so if you have one you will be alone. Camping there is a true pleasure. Sitting at Cape Final for a sunset, watching the shadows grow long and the lights blink on atop the South Rim, is an experience that's hard to match. There are no official tent sites, so it is up to you to choose one. The bumpy rocks along the ridges make for an uncomfortable choice, but most of the woods are quite flat and sheltered from the wind. Watch out for cacti (the smaller ones are often hidden). Because there are no water sources, you will need to bring your own water for cooking and drinking. Keep in mind that it can get chilly at Cape Final, even in July. If you go, make sure you bring some warm clothes. While you're there, be sure to bag and hang your food, dishes, and toothpaste where animals can't get to them.

7 WIDFORSS POINT TRAIL

Highly Recommended

SUMMARY

The Widforss Trail takes you deep into the forests of the Widforss peninsula and ends with a fine view into the Grand Canyon. For a lover of flowers and woodland scenery, it has few rivals on the North Rim. This trail is suitable for both day and overnight hikers.

TRAIL INFORMATION	WIDFORSS POINT TRAIL

DISTANCE 10 miles round-trip   **DIFFICULTY** Easy

APPROXIMATE HIKING TIME 6 hours

TRAIL CONDITION Good, unmaintained

WATER AVAILABILITY No water

ELEVATION CHANGE 400 feet

WIDFORSS POINT

0 — 1 MILES 2 — 3

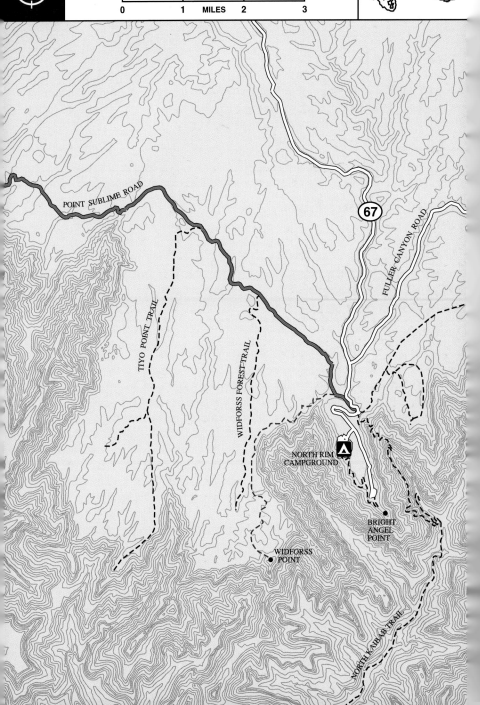

POINT SUBLIME ROAD

67

FULLER CANYON ROAD

TIYO POINT TRAIL

WIDFORSS FOREST TRAIL

NORTH RIM
CAMPGROUND

BRIGHT
ANGEL
POINT

WIDFORSS
POINT

NORTH KAIBAB TRAIL

N

WIDFORSS POINT TRAIL

PARKING
There is a parking area next to the trailhead.

TRAILHEAD
From Grand Canyon Lodge, drive north on AZ 67 for about 2.5 miles until you see a sign for the turnoff to Widforss Point. Turn left onto the curving dirt road and follow it for about a half mile. There is a signed parking area for the Widforss Trail on the left. The trail leaves the south side of the parking lot.

NOTES
There is a small dispenser offering pamphlets for a self-guided nature walk over the first two miles of the trail. They cost a quarter (on the honor system) and are worth it.

TRAIL DESCRIPTION
From the trailhead the trail swings uphill with a small ponderosa valley below you to the left. In this stretch it feels as if you are in the Rockies, climbing cool piney mountains. You come back to Arizona when the trail reaches the rim, providing you with your first views into the Transept. The trail switches back from here and descends into the woods a short distance before climbing back to the rim. This pattern continues for the next two miles, with the trail following the rim for the most part but regularly dipping back into the trees. Working around streambeds instead of dropping into them, the trail stays quite flat.

You'll see several numbered wooden pegs in the ground for the first half of the Widforss trail. These mark points of interest and are deciphered by the numbers in the pamphlet available at the trailhead. Notable among them are 9 (petrified reptile tracks) and 10 (a gigantic old-growth ponderosa pine, perhaps 500 years old).

The trail along the rim has several side trails to viewpoints on the left. These are fairly similar, but worth checking out. Many of the side trails lead back around to the main trail and are nice places to enjoy a break looking out into the Transept.

Two and a half miles from the start, the trail swings south and leaves the rim to run through the woods. The rest of the path runs through the familiar North Rim landscape of evergreens and aspens interspersed with fire burned trunks. Between lightning and forest fires the trees of the North Rim have burned many times. A few sections of the forest are almost entirely burnt trees. The ground is pitted with holes, some of them still containing black stumpy remnants of the trees that once grew here, but there are many wildflowers as well. Beds of purple lupines blanket the ground beneath the trees, with desert paintbrushes springing up around them.

The trail runs on to the south, bending through the trees. For the most part it's flat with a few mild ups and downs. At length you begin to see the horizon through the trees, and the trail narrows as it reaches the end. There is a picnic table and some clear spaces that make for good tent sites near the end of the trail. The viewpoint is a short distance farther along the trail on a rock ledge to the right. The trail itself turns left and circles back around the campsite to form a quarter-mile loop.

8 POWELL PLATEAU TRAIL
Recommended

SUMMARY

The Powell Plateau, a broad shoulder of land to the west of the North Rim, provides one of the most remote and rewarding day hikes in the canyon. The trail takes you into a secluded woodland amidst sweeping views of the northern canyon.

TRAIL INFORMATION	POWELL PLATEAU TRAIL

DISTANCE 6–12 miles round-trip   **DIFFICULTY** Moderate

APPROXIMATE HIKING TIME 3–5 hours

TRAIL CONDITION Fair, unmaintained

WATER AVAILABILITY No water

ELEVATION CHANGE 1700 feet

POWELL PLATEAU

0   .5   MILES   1   1.5

NEWBERRY
POINT

POWELL PLATEAU

MUAV
SADDLE

SWAMP
POINT

NORTH BASS TRAIL

DUTTON
POINT

MASONIC
TEMPLE

WALTHENBERG CANYON

HAKATAI CANYON

POWELL PLATEAU TRAIL

PARKING
There is a parking area near the trailhead.

TRAILHEAD
Getting to the Powell Plateau trailhead isn't easy. The roads that lead there, particularly the last eight miles, are quite poor, and four-wheel drive is required. The roads referred to here are all dirt forest roads, and their numbers should be indicated at intersections by wooden stakes. From the Grand Canyon Lodge, drive north on AZ-67. Four miles past the park entrance station, turn left (west) onto Forest Road 22 (a mile south of Kaibab Lodge). Drive 2.1 miles and turn left on 270 at a four-way intersection. Drive 2.3 miles and turn right on 223. Drive 5.8 miles and take a hard left on 268. After 0.3 miles bear left on 268 B and drive nine miles.

The first 1.2 miles on 268 B aren't much worse than the bumpy roads you've been driving on, but the next 7.8 miles are very bad and require a sturdy vehicle. Continue straight on this road until you come to a wider space to park in. There's a wonderful view of Muav Canyon to the left and a tentsite nearby. Although the road continues for another quarter mile, it's not worth driving. The road ends at Swamp Point, the official trailhead. There's a large water container here (used to fight forest fires) and an informative NPS sign for the trailhead is straight ahead.

NOTES
Although the Powell Plateau trail is short, a longer backpack to fully explore the area is also a good option provided you carry in enough water.

TRAIL DESCRIPTION
For the first three-quarters of a mile down to the Muav Saddle (900 feet of descent) you are on the North Bass Trail, which shares the same trailhead as the Powell Plateau Trail. The uneven and rocky trail descends a little to the left, passing through scrub oak and pines on a long traverse around a shoulder of land. Saddle Canyon and Steamboat Mountain are spread out below you to the right. After descending gently for a third of a mile, the trail switches back to the left for an even longer traverse back towards Muav Canyon. From here you can see the trail running up the side of Powell Plateau. After a half mile you descend abruptly on a series of fairly steep switchbacks. Soon you will reach the trees of Muav Saddle. The trail is a little overgrown, but not terribly difficult.

There is a four-way intersection at Muav Saddle. The North Bass Trail drops down to the left on its way to the Colorado River, and a short spur trail to Muav Cabin goes off to the right. The cabin was formerly used by the Park Service and is available for hikers to stay in overnight. The Powell Plateau Trail continues on and soon begins to climb the Plateau. Shortly past the saddle the trail swings left (uphill)

and the trail becomes very overgrown. After walking through some large pines the trail cuts left, working along the side of a wash before curving right at the wash's center. It traverses in this direction for a quarter mile and then switches back and forth as it ascends the plateau.

After a half mile of climbing, the plateau evens out and the trail becomes straighter and gentler in grade. It passes through thorny scrubland toward the trees on the flat summit of the plateau. For the next three quarters of a mile the trail is flat, winding through open ponderosa woods full of gigantic trees. The trail nears the rim twice, and the view of the main canyon is fantastic. At times, especially toward the end, the trail is faint and difficult to make out. It ends abruptly near the start of Dutton Canyon. On the rim to your left, the rocky ledges make for a great resting spot with spectacular views.

Bushwhacking through the flat, open forest of Powell Plateau can be very rewarding, as long as you have a good map and are experienced in such endeavors. Six miles from the trailhead is Dutton Point. Work your way along the rim to get there.

DUTTON POINT WAS JOHN WESLEY POWELL'S FAVORITE VIEWPOINT INTO THE GRAND CANYON

You may come across some Ancestral Puebloan ruins in the course of your wanderings—hundreds of Ancestral Puebloans lived at this spot around in the 11th century. There are over 80 Ancestral Puebloan sites recorded on Powell Plateau.

9 NORTH KAIBAB TRAIL
Recommended

SUMMARY

The only maintained trail on the North Rim that reaches the Colorado River. From start to finish, the trail passes through more geological and ecological zones than any other trail in the canyon. Although strenuous, it is a beautiful path well equipped with modern facilities. Highlights include tunnels, waterfalls, rock monoliths, and deep dark canyons.

TRAIL INFORMATION	NORTH KAIBAB TRAIL
DISTANCE 28 miles round-trip	**DIFFICULTY** Strenuous
APPROXIMATE HIKING TIME 3–4 days	
TRAIL CONDITION Excellent, maintained	
WATER AVAILABILITY Piped in water available along the trail	
ELEVATION CHANGE 5,855 feet	

N. KAIBAB TRAIL

0 — 1 — MILES 2 — 3

SUPAI TUNNEL
ROARING SPRINGS
BRIGHT ANGEL POINT
TIYO POINT
WIDFORSS POINT
COTTONWOOD CAMPGROUND
SHIVA TEMPLE
MANU TEMPLE
RIBBON FALLS
BUDDHA TEMPLE
ISIS TEMPLE
BRAHMA TEMPLE
TOWER OF SET
CHEOPS PYRAMID
THE BOX
ZOROASTER TEMPLE
PHANTOM RANCH
23
BRIGHT ANGEL CAMPGROUND
CLEAR CREEK TRAIL
PLATEAU POINT
TONTO TRAIL
MOHAVE POINT
BRIGHT ANGEL TRAIL
22
YAVAPAI POINT
24
SOUTH KAIBAB TRAIL
YAKI POINT
64

NORTH KAIBAB TRAIL

DAY HIKES
Coconino Overlook: 1.5 miles round-trip
Supai Tunnel: 4 miles round-trip
Roaring Springs: 9.4 miles round-trip

PARKING
There is a parking lot next to the trailhead. During peak season, the lot often fills up early, but a daily shuttle runs between the parking lot and the Grand Canyon Lodge (inquire at the lodge for details).

TRAILHEAD
The North Kaibab trailhead is located two miles north of Grand Canyon Lodge on the east side of AZ-67. To get to the start of the trail, head toward the mule pens at the top of the parking lot and take a hard right down the broad, sandy trail hemmed in by two rows of logs.

NOTES
Mule trains are common on the North Kaibab Trail. If you see a mule train approaching, move to the inside of the trail and obey instructions from the mule wrangler. The steepest section of the North Kaibab Trail lies between the trailhead and Roaring Springs, dropping 3,600 feet in 4.7 miles. If you are hiking the entire trail, two days each way is recommended. Backpackers are restricted to staying in developed campgrounds. There are two campgrounds on the trail: Cottonwood (6.9 miles) and Bright Angel (14.4 miles). Piped water is available at Supai Tunnel (1.8 miles), Roaring Springs, Cottonwood Campground, and Bright Angel Campground. Bright Angel Creek is a perennial water supply, but must be treated before drinking. The water at Supai Tunnel and Roaring Springs is usually turned off in early October. The water at Cottonwood is usually left on until Thanksgiving.

TRAIL DESCRIPTION
From the trailhead, the North Kaibab Trail slopes down a gentle grade through a forest of ponderosa pine, white fir, Douglas fir, and quaking aspen. Soon the trail reaches a series of switchbacks. About a mile from the top, Coconino Overlook opens out over Roaring Spring Canyon.

From the overlook, the trail descends on switchbacks through Roaring Spring Canyon. Eventually, at 1.8 miles, you reach Supai Tunnel. A seasonal water faucet and three toilet stalls are located shortly before the entrance.

Supai Tunnel is a worthwhile destination for a day hike. The tunnel is about 20 feet long and tall enough for a mule with a rider. Once through the tunnel, you are treated to a fine view of imposing cliffs (above you to the right) streaked pink, yellow, and blue—looking more like modern art than rock walls.

Supai Tunnel

On the other side of Supai Tunnel, the vegetation becomes typical of the pinyon-juniper life zone. As you drop into the heart of Roaring Springs Canyon, the trail becomes a little less sandy and the switchbacks become more intense. The trail works along a wide ledge on the eastern side of the gorge before reaching Redwall Bridge, which takes you to the western side of the canyon. The trail climbs briefly before leveling out to a mild descent. The ledge works its way around the dramatic curves in the cliffs, with Roaring Canyon plunging away from the trail's edge. Soon, a striking rocky spire called the "Needle" rises to the left of the trail.

The trail winds along the western wall of the canyon, with some switchbacks along particularly sheer sections. As you approach Roaring Springs, you'll be able to see a cascading waterfall bursting forth from the rock on the far side of the canyon. Soon you'll reach a signed junction with a side trail leading to Roaring Springs. Roaring Springs is a scenic place filled with cottonwoods and greenery. The side trail that leads there is about a quarter of a mile long with an elevation loss of roughly 100 feet. There is a bathroom nearby and a faucet with drinking water.

As the main trail continues past the Roaring Springs junction, it passes the residence of the Roaring Springs pumphouse operator before crossing a bridge that spans Bright Angel Creek. The trail is now entering the Lower Sonoran Desert Zone, and plants such as yucca and Engelmann prickly pear cactus start to appear. The trail follows the eastern side of Bright Angel Canyon for 1.4 miles, undulating up and down mildly before reaching Cottonwood Campground.

Cottonwood is a pleasant place—not quite as shady as the name implies, but cooler than the rest of the desert. Toilets and drinking water are available from May through October. Campsites include a picnic table, two metal boxes for food storage, and a T-bar you can use to hang packs or laundry from (the T-bar used to be used for hanging food, but local critters have figured out how to climb the smooth metal pole). Cottonwood's views of Oza Butte and Bright Angel Point are impressive. At night,

ROARING SPRINGS

Roaring Springs is the main water source for the North Rim, the South Rim, and Phantom Ranch. A pump lifts the water over 3,600 feet to the North Rim, and a trans-canyon pipeline carries the rest to Phantom Ranch and the South Rim. About a half-mile from Roaring Springs is the residence of the NPS employee who manages the pump house. The current pump house manager has lived at Roaring Springs for over 30 years. He raised his children in the canyon and gets his groceries delivered via helicopter.

The Zuni Indians trace their origins to Ribbon Falls...

Ribbon Falls

you can often see the lights of the Grand Canyon Lodge.

Past the campground the trail continues to follow the eastern side of Bight Angel Creek. About a half mile from the campground the trail crosses Wall Creek, and after another half mile you'll reach the side trail to Ribbon Falls. Ribbon falls is one of the most popular sights on the North Kaibab Trail. The side trail leading there is a quarter mile long. It crosses over a small bridge, runs along a stream, and clambers over some rocks before opening up onto a hidden grotto with a 100-foot waterfall. Ribbon Falls was named by early surveyor François Matthes, who thought the water from the falls resembled ribbons blowing in the breeze. The top of the falls spills about 40 feet onto a moss covered travertine cone. Maidenhair fern, golden columbine, and scarlet monkeyflower thrive here. There's a trail to the left that takes you above the moss and behind the falls. Another trail leads up to a rocky alcove far to the right. (Be careful on both of these trails, the drop-off is steep and the trails can get slippery.) With its tranquil atmosphere and cooling sprays, Ribbon Falls is an excellent place to spend a hot summer afternoon if you're hiking between Bright Angel Campground and Cotton-wood Campground. (Note: Although there is another trail leading back to the

Right: Cooling off under the moss

North Kaibab Trail from the Ribbon Falls, it can get tricky and is best avoided.) From the Ribbon Falls junction, the North Kaibab Trail ascends a series of steep switchbacks for a quarter of a mile before falling back into its typical descent. The trail runs along the creek for the next mile and a half, with an unavoidable wet swampy area towards the end of this stretch.

Past the marshy swamp, the trail enters the awe inspiring four-mile corridor known as The Box. Made of 1.7 billion year-old Vishnu Schist and Zoroaster Granite, the walls of The Box tower above you as you walk between them. In places, the walls are over 1,000 feet high. As a result, much of this section is covered in shade for long periods of time. The Box has a primeval feel. Its twists and turns shut out the rest of the world, leaving behind only the sounds of rushing water and chirping birds. Bird watchers will definitely want their binoculars out here. There are four bridges that criss cross the Box, but for the most part the trail follows the eastern side. After the fourth bridge, the path spills out into a more open area, becoming a little sunnier as it heads three quarters of a mile towards Phantom Ranch.

The buildings at Phantom Ranch line the trail for half a mile, luring hikers with air conditioning and cold beer. Bright Angel Campground is located farther down the trail. Bright Angel Campground has the same amenities as Cottonwood, but is always more crowded. The tent sites are located on the right hand side of the cool and refreshing waters of Bright Angel Creek. Overheated hikers love to wade in the creek for extended periods of time, especially in the summer months when temperatures top 100 degrees. In the evening, Phantom Ranch offers ranger programs. (Note: Bright Angel Campground has many animals that have grown quite bold in their campsite expeditions. Be careful with your food and never feed the animals.)

The trail to the Colorado River is another quarter mile down the left hand side of Bright Angel Creek. You can cross the river on one of two impressive bridges. If you haven't hiked enough already, you can loop between the two bridges along the South Kaibab Trail, which features some extensive Anasazi ruins on its north side.

For a return trip in the summer, start very early in the morning, well before sunrise if possible. It will be much cooler during this time, making the strenuous hike back much more pleasant.

BRIGHT ANGEL CREEK

Bright Angel Creek was named by John Wesley Powell in 1874. He originally named it Silver Creek, but later changed the name in the published account of his Colorado River expedition. "The little affluent which we have discovered here," he wrote, "is a clear, beautiful creek, or river, as it would be termed in this western country, where streams are not abundant. We have named one stream, away above, in honor of the great chief of the 'Bad Angels,' [Dirty Devil Creek] and as this is a beautiful contrast to that, we conclude to name it 'Bright Angel.'"

Bright Angel Creek

Thunder River Falls

10 *THUNDER RIVER TRAIL*

Highly Recommended

SUMMARY

The Thunder River Trail is a challenging multi-day route that descends nearly 6,000 feet to the Colorado River. The scenery is amazing but due to the trail's isolation, steep scrambles, and river crossings it should only be attempted by experienced backpackers. The Deer Creek trail is a spectacular offshoot of the Thunder River Trail.

TRAIL INFORMATION	THUNDER RIVER TRAIL

DISTANCE 24-30 miles round-trip   **DIFFICULTY** Very Strenuous

APPROXIMATE HIKING TIME 3-4 days

TRAIL CONDITION Fair, unmaintained

WATER AVAILABILITY Thunder River, Deer Creek

ELEVATION CHANGE 6650 feet

THUNDER RIVER

N

0   1   MILES   2   3

232

INDIAN HOLLOW

GRAND CANYON N.P.

THUNDER RIVER TRAIL

292A

BILL HALL TRAIL

MONUMENT POINT

THE ESPLANADE

DEER CREEK TRAIL

THRONE ROOM

THUNDER RIVER FALLS

DEER CREEK FALLS

UPPER TAPEATS CAMPGROUND

LOWER TAPEATS CAMPGROUND

TAPEATS CREEK

TAPEATS TERRACE

THUNDER RIVER TRAIL

PARKING

There is a parking area next to the trailhead.

TRAILHEAD

The first challenge of the Thunder River Trail is getting there. The trailhead at Monument Point is at the end of a confusing network of forest roads. From Grand Canyon Lodge, drive north on AZ-67. Four miles past the park entrance station, turn left (west) onto Forest Road 22 (1 mile south of Kaibab Lodge). Although the roads are dirt from this point on, most cars should be able to handle them. Drive 11 miles on road 22, passing Dry Park fire tower. When you come to a T intersection, turn left onto road 206. Drive 6 miles and take a right onto road 214. Drive 3 miles and bear right on to road 272. Drive 6 miles and turn right at the T intersection onto road 292. There will be a sign to go straight 2 miles for Monument Point. Go straight, then turn onto road 292A. Drive 4 miles to the Bill Hall trailhead, a large open space with a gate at the end. Although it begins at 7000 feet (as opposed to 6250 for the Thunder River Trailhead), the Bill Hall Trail takes five miles off of your trip to Surprise Valley or Tapeats Creek. It is recommended if you're going to Tapeats Creek or the Colorado.

NOTES

There is no water between Monument Point and Thunder River. If you're backpacking you'll want to cache a few gallons on the Esplanade for the return trip. Camping at large is legal anywhere between the trailhead and about 1.5 miles north of Upper Tapeats campsite. In the summer, the trail is sometimes closed due to extreme heat. If you are here in the summer, carry extra water and bring a water filter or iodine to safely replenish your water supply.

TRAIL DESCRIPTION

After hiking through the trailhead gate, pass the forest road to your right and turn left by the NPS information sign. The trail immediately climbs through a scorched landscape of burned out trees—the result of a 1996 wildfire touched off by lightning. The trail follows the rim for three quarters of a mile, passing several fine viewpoints along the way. Soon the trail splits, with one branch heading left to a viewpoint and the other continuing to the right. Both branches rejoin not long after the fork.

The trail eventually crests a hill and continues, quite flat, for another three quarters of a mile. A cairn marks the spot near the tip of Monument Point where the trail leaves the rim behind and dives down into the canyon. At this point the trail becomes crumbly and challenging. Careful footing is a must. The trail switches back and forth a few times down the steep, rocky slope. After descending a few hundred feet, the trail veers right as it traverses the slope. As it wraps around the ridge, the beautiful expanse of red slickrock known as the Esplanade spreads out below you.

Along the traverse there are several sections of alarming exposure to steep cliffs. When you finally reach the end of the traverse, there will be a relatively difficult descent/scramble of about 10 feet. If your packs are heavy you may want to ferry them down before descending yourself. A short rope to lower your packs can be handy here.

At the end of the traverse is a mile-long stretch of switchbacks through pinyon-juniper woodlands. Although quite steep at first, the slope of the land becomes gentler and gentler as you drop towards the Esplanade. The trail then runs at a fairly smooth grade through scrub and sagebrush terrain before intersecting the Thunder River Trail. There is a small sign in the ground indicating that the Indian Hollow Trailhead is to your right and Thunder River is to your left. Bear left at the junction and head southeast.

The next 2.5 miles of the trail passes through the Esplanade and is well marked by small cairns. For the most part the trail is very easy to follow, although there may be moments of uncertainty. Pay close attention to where you're going. As the Esplanade slopes down, the trail picks its way through several unique rock formations with panoramic views unfolding below.

Soon, you'll reach the southern rim of the Esplanade. At this point the trail descends, switching back and forth along a steep rocky slope. The footing is uneven in places, but sturdy rock walls guard the sides of the trail. The trail's descent continues for about a mile and a half until you reach Surprise Valley.

The trail through Surprise Valley is flat and clear as it winds through the desert scrub. After approximately one mile the Deer Creek Trail veers off to the right

(there's no sign, only a split in the dirt paths). Take the left fork to get to Thunder River. After another mile, you'll be able to hear the waterfall that marks the start of Thunder River. The path then descends 1500 feet in a steady stream of switchbacks. Half a mile down, there's a short side trail that leads to the edge of the waterfall.

The waterfall is a sight to behold. Bursting forth from a limestone cave, it cascades down the parched terrain and supports a dense corridor of lush vegetation on both sides—cottonwoods, maidenhair fern, and monkeyflower thrive here. On a hot summer day, the spray near the falls is fantastically refreshing.

After the waterfall, the main trail continues down on switchbacks to where Thunder River flows into Tapeats Creek. Soon, the trail passes through Upper Tapeats campsite.

Past the campsite, the trail consists of a series of exposed ledge walks, bushwhacks through thorny vegetation, and tricky river crossings. Depending on the spring runoff, Tapeats creek can be extremely hazardous—in a heavy snow year it can be almost impossible to cross the river due to high water. Do not take this trail unless you have plenty of time and the necessary expertise to safely navigate through such unfriendly terrain. The challenge can be fun, but it is a real challenge. After the last stream crossing, the path climbs gradually to a high side canyon rim hundreds of feet above the water. The trail is good here and the view of the creek emptying into the Colorado is impressive. The sandy beach that makes up Lower Tapeats is a peaceful, isolated oasis among steep canyon walls.

Right: Taking in the view at Thunder River Falls

Throne Room

DEER CREEK NARROWS
Offshoot of Thunder River Trail, Highly Recommended

DEER CREEK NARROWS

The Deer Creek Trail is a spectacular 6 mile round-trip offshoot of the Thunder River Trail. It starts at the junction with the Thunder River Trail in Surprise Valley (see preceding trail description). After the junction, the trail descends until it reaches a large jumble of gray rocks with views of Deer Creek in the valley below. The trail then traverses a ledge to the right, swings around to the left, and drops down to a secluded waterfall bursting forth through the Muav Limestone. A small trail leads to an open space behind the falls.

On the other side of the waterfall is a shaded alcove known as the Throne Room. Scattered throughout this open space are large slabs of rocks that have been arranged into surprisingly comfortable throne-like seats.

After leaving the Throne Room, the trail continues its descent until it reaches Deer Creek. After crossing the creek—the best crossing is a little to the left of where the trail hits the water—the trail continues along the southern bank, passing through giant reed grass and over some scattered rocks. Soon the creek tumbles down into beautiful Deer Creek Narrows. The trail runs at the same level as Deer Creek a short distance before plunging into Deer Creek Narrows. The serpentine rock walls of Deer Creek Narrows have been gracefully carved out of Tapeats Sandstone, twisting up and around you with the creek rushing below. Along the walls next to the trail are

Throne Room waterfall

Deer Creek Narrows

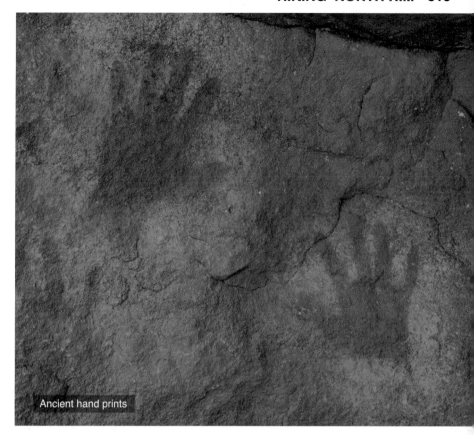
Ancient hand prints

handprints painted on by the Indians that used to inhabit this part of the Grand Canyon. They were created by blowing white pigment around a flat hand placed against the wall, most likely with a hollow reed or piece of bone. Enjoy, but do not touch.

The path follows the right hand side of the creek, and is very safe in all but a few places. After passing through Deer Creek Narrows, the trail reaches a stunning overlook high above the Colorado River. From here the trail turns right and works its way down to the river. After switching back and forth, the trail emerges near the river. There is some poison ivy here, so be careful.

Deer Creek emerges from Deer Creek Narrows in a spectacular hundred-foot waterfall that comes crashing down from the slot canyon above. Deer Creek Falls is the largest waterfall visible from the Colorado River in the Grand Canyon. Alongside the falls is a shallow but refreshing swimming hole. This area is extremely popular with river trips in the summer. The misty wind of the falls stings as you approach it and the roar of the water crashing down is deafening. A rainbow often appears in the mist surrounding the base of Deer Creek Falls, creating a spectacular finale to a long day trekking across Surprise Valley.

LOOP WALK

For those who don't wish to retrace their steps back up Deer Creek, there is an unofficial, unnamed trail back more or less along the Colorado to Lower Tapeats. It's about four miles long. It is not recommended for anyone without good route-finding skills. To get there, return to the start of the narrows, cross them before the creek drops below the trail, and climb the scrubby slope ahead of you. When you reach the saddle, you'll be able to see the faint dirt trail snaking away on the other side. The path is fairly clear and consistent, running a few hundred feet above the River for about two miles before dropping down to the Colorado. The higher part of the path from Deer Creek towards Tapeats Creek is among the wildest, grandest, and most isolated routes north of the river. When in doubt, stay high—the descent to the river is very clear. The trail continues along the rocky beach, marked erratically by cairns. Take care during this section, as the path grows fainter. There are a few simple scrambles on the way. After another two miles you will get to Tapeats Creek. It's the next big stream entering the Colorado after Deer Creek and is difficult to mistake. From Lower Tapeats Creek take the Thunder River Trail back to the campsite.

Deer Creek Falls

HAVASU

Havasu Falls

HAVASU CANYON

TO GRAND CANYON visitors in the know, the name Havasu conjures up images of a remote desert paradise. Everyone agrees that this secluded side canyon, located 100 miles west of the South Rim, is one of the most beautiful—and unexpected—places in America. For over 700 years, Havasu Canyon has been the home of the Havasupai Indians, whose name means "People of the Blue-Green Water." A short distance from the Havasupai village of Supai, located in the heart of the canyon 2,000 feet below the rim, are two of the most beautiful waterfalls in the world: Havasu Falls (100 feet) and Mooney Falls (196 feet). The lure of these waterfalls is so powerful that, despite their remote location, they draw roughly 35,000 visitors a year—a number strictly limited by the Havasupai.

Although Havasu Canyon only receives nine inches of rain a year, it drains a 3,000 square-mile basin. That's enough to create a perennial stream flowing through the canyon at about 38 million gallons a day. Even more impressive, the stream tumbles down the canyon in a series of beautiful pools and waterfalls. The color of the water—an unearthly blue rarely seen outside the Caribbean—is caused by a light coating of travertine (calcium carbonate) on the riverbed.

Getting to Havasu isn't easy. After driving for miles along the remote roads of the Havasupai Indian Reservation, you'll reach Hualapi Hilltop, where all visitors must leave their cars. All visitors must also have advance reservations to visit Supai. There are no roads to Supai—it is only accessible by foot, helicopter, or mule. (Supai is the town in the United States where daily mail is still delivered by mule.) As a result, the village remains sheltered from much of the modern world. In many ways Havasu Canyon seems like the land that time forgot. The roughly 500 Havasupai still living in Supai continue to speak their native tongue, horses and dogs freely roam the dirt roads, and illumination is only provided by the sun. All this, combined with the stunning natural scenery, creates a vacation experience like no other.

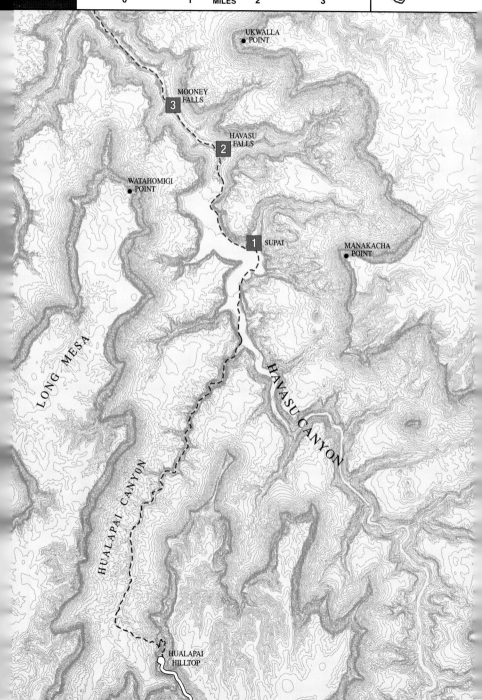

HAVASU

N

0　　　　1　MILES　2　　　　3

UKWALLA
POINT

MOONEY
FALLS
3

HAVASU
FALLS
2

WATAHOMIGI
POINT

1 SUPAI

MANAKACHA
POINT

LONG MESA

HAVASU CANYON

HUALAPAI CANYON

HUALAPAI
HILLTOP

HAVASU BASICS

GETTING TO HAVASU

The most popular trail leading to Supai begins on Hualapai Hilltop. (For the closest lodging to Hualapai Hilltop, visit destinationpress.com.) To get there take AZ-66 off I-40 and head toward Peach Springs. Six miles east of Peach Springs turn onto Indian Route Highway 18 and follow it 56 miles to Hualapai Hilltop.

ON FOOT — The trail from Hualapai Hilltop to Supai is eight miles (plan on about three hours to hike down, four hours to hike back). The switchbacks near the top of the trail are strenuous, but the rest of the trail is not hard, although sandy, and easy to follow.

BY MULE — A ride to Supai from Hualapai Hilltop costs $70 per person one-way, $120 per person round-trip (reservations: 928-448-2111). A ride to the campground cost $75 per person one-way, $150 round-trip (reservations: 928-448-2121).

BY HELICOPTER — Skydance Helicopters (800-882-1651) runs a shuttle between Hualapai Hilltop and Supai for $70 per person one-way. Papillon Helicopters (928-638-2419) runs a service from Tusayan for around $450 per person round-trip.

CAMPING & LODGING

There's a small lodge in Supai that offers plain rooms with air conditioning and private bathrooms. For reservations call 928-448-2111. Note: Between May and October, the lodge is usually booked months in advance. The campground at Havasu, located 2 miles beyond Supai near the waterfalls, accommodates about 200 people. Reservations are required (928-448-2141) and are usually easy to come by except during the peak summer season and on holiday weekends.

PERMITS & FEES

All visitors to Havasu Canyon must pay a $20 entrance fee. If you are staying at the lodge, this fee is automatically added to your bill. Campers should pay the fee at the tourist office in Supai.

FOOD & DINING

The only dining option in Supai is the town cafe, which serves cafeteria-style food. A general store in Supai also sells basic snacks.

Supai Lodge

1 SUPAI VILLAGE

In the 1930s an anthropologist visiting Supai remarked that it was "the only spot in the United States where native culture has remained in anything like its pristine condition." Although modernization has since come to Supai in the form of electricity, telephones, and the Internet, the pace of life remains markedly different from the rest of the United States—and the Havasupai like it that way. Any suggestion of building a road into the canyon has always been rejected.

The earliest residents of Havasu Canyon were an ancient culture known as the Cohonina. It is not known if the Havasupai are descendents of the Cohonina or are an entirely separate group, but by A.D. 1300 the Havasupai had firmly established themselves in Havasu Canyon. Still, the Havasupai only lived there during the warm summer growing season. In the winter, when the tall walls of Havasu Canyon only let in about five hours of sunlight a day, the Havasupai would move above the rim where game and firewood were more abundant.

In 1776 a Spanish missionary named Tomas Garces became the first white man to set eyes on Havasu Canyon. American prospectors arrived several decades later, but the biggest threat to the Havasupai came in 1866 when Congress granted much of their lands to the Atlantic and Pacific Railroad. Following years of dispute, the Havasupai moved onto a reservation in Havasu Canyon that was less than one square mile in size. Finally, after much legal wrangling, the Havasupai Reservation was expanded to its present size of 185,000 acres in 1975.

2 HAVASU FALLS

Havasu Falls is located two miles past Supai. To get there, follow the dirt path that heads down the canyon (really just an extension of the main road). After a mile and a half you'll reach Navajo Falls. Although it's the first major waterfall, Navajo Falls is not much more than a small cascade over an overgrown cliff.

Another half mile brings you to Havasu Falls. As the trail starts to descend along the western canyon wall, Havasu Falls makes a sudden and spectacular appearance to your right. At this point you are at eye level with the top of the 100-foot falls. Following the trail farther down will bring you to several well-trodden side trails that lead to the beach area. Although crowded in the summer, this is one of the most magical swimming holes in North America.

A century ago, Havasu Falls was a much different waterfall than the one you see today. Back then, Havasu Creek cascaded over much of the wall in a wide curtain of water, explaining the overhanging sheets of built-up travertine next to the falls. Then, several decades ago, a flash flood roared through Havasu Canyon and knocked out a large notch in the wall. Suddenly, the creek was channeled into a much narrower—and much more spectacular—waterfall. But flash floods giveth, and flash floods taketh away. In 1993 another flash flood destroyed several travertine terraces at the base of the falls that had built up to form a series of beautiful cascading pools (famous in many pre-1993 photographs). Note: Because Havasu Canyon drains such a large area, flash floods are a constant threat, see p.23.

3   MOONEY FALLS

Mooney Falls is the tallest waterfall in Havasu Canyon. At 196 feet it's taller than Niagra Falls. To get there, follow the main path one mile past Havasu Falls. This will bring you to a stunning overlook. Reaching the base of the falls, however, is much more difficult—you'll have to descend a steep and slippery path that is not for the faint of heart. Use extreme caution if you choose this route. Once down, the trail continues past the base of Mooney Falls, but becomes very rugged from this point on.

The Havasupai consider this to be their most sacred waterfall. They call it Mother of the Waters. The name Mooney Falls is derived from a tragic death that occurred here in 1880. In that year, a group of American prospectors descended Havasu Canyon in the hopes of finding gold. When they reached the Mother of the Waters, they could go no farther. At that time, the trail to the base of the falls did not exist. According to the Havasupai, who accompanied the prospectors to the falls, no man had ever passed beyond this point, only the "birds of the air or spirits of the dead." Undeterred, a prospector named Daniel Mooney decided to be lowered down by rope. With a rope tied around his waist, a group of miners and Havasupai lowered him over the falls, but his rope soon became stuck in a jagged crevice. As the men tried to free the rope, it began to fray. Suddenly, the rope snapped and Mooney fell to his death. Unable to reach their friend, the prospectors were forced to return 10 months later. They built a ladder down to the base of the falls, but by that time Mooney's body was encrusted in a fresh layer of travertine. He was buried where he lay.

Mooney Falls

INDEX